A HIST
DREAMS

A HISTORY OF DREAMS

A. J. J. RATCLIFF

SENATE

A History of Dreams

First published in 1923 by Grant Richards & Co, London.

This edition first published in 1996 by Senate, an imprint of
Random House UK Ltd, Random House, 20 Vauxhall Bridge
Road, London SW1V 2SA

Copyright © A. J. J. Ratcliff 1923

ISBN 1 85958 168 4

Printed and bound in Guernsey by The Guernsey Press Co. Ltd

INTRODUCTION

My sole excuse for yielding to the author's invitation to write this introduction is the very great interest I have felt in reading the manuscript, for I cannot claim to be in the slightest degree competent to discuss its subject scientifically. The real reason I fear would be discovered by an expert psychoanalyst to be one of self-conceit, for I confess to feelings of that nature when Mr. Ratcliff tells me that it was from chance remarks in one of my lectures, eight or nine years ago, that the idea of this work arose.

My interest in the book will be in one sense shared, I feel confident, by every reader; interest in the skill with which the argument is expounded, and pleasure at having such wide reading so ably and appetisingly laid before one. Seldom, I imagine, has the Freudian theory of the dream been so attractively presented as in the Addisonian myth of the offspring of Mr. Love-in-early-infancy and Seeing-an-old-sweetheart disguised as a ballroom slipper. And the, to me, quite novel analogy between the unconscious in words and the unconscious which wells up into our dreams, as exemplified in the American slang extract, is not only interesting but possibly of great practical importance.

In another sense my interest is unique and peculiar to myself, and cannot be shared; yet each reader will have his own corresponding interest as each has his own memories and sentiments. For I felt as I read that the author was making an appeal to a deeper self than my conscious workaday mind. And some of the explanation rushed into my consciousness when on page 111, I chanced on the word " Crusoe." For I realized then quite suddenly that something in Mr. Ratcliff's style was reminding me of Robinson Crusoe, and was tapping joys and fears I had experienced in early boyhood when reading Defoe's masterpiece. I trembled again for a moment at Crusoe's vision in his own dream (which I recalled for the first time for very many years and yet could turn to at once in my old copy, still preserved) and saw again with him a man descend from a great black cloud in a bright flame of fire, and heard his terrible voice. And scenes from " The Pilgrim's Progress," read at the same period, also came back to me with much clearness and great emotional coloring, and I recalled how they had formed the material of my daydreams and how I had in all reality feared to find chained lions in my path on the stair landing, or a real load of sin growing on my shoulders. Every one must, I feel sure, have similar childhood memories which sometimes break through into consciousness and which, since they then have strong emotional effects, probably have an influence on character and temperament even while yet submerged in the unconscious. Daydreams and the real world are curiously intermingled for the imaginative child, who sees " a tree full of angels at Peckham," as readily as a field of buttercups; and I often think that the material with which we nourish those daydreams — fairy tales, myths, " Alice in Wonderland," " The Blue Bird," — must have an influence on character we hardly know of. Has any one suffered Mary Rose's fate from dreaming of Peter Pan, or is it, on the contrary, more likely that some have escaped it from having Peter Pan as an outlet?

The stuff that dreams are made of is the stuff that molds character, and no study can be more necessary. Mr. Ratcliff's contribution to that study is literary rather than experimental, but is not the less important. Above all it is eminently enjoyable.

GODFREY H. THOMSON,
Newcastle-on-Tyne.

December, 1921

A History of Dreams

CHAPTER I

THE CHARACTERISTICS OF DREAMS

> " We are such stuff
> As dreams are made on; and our little life
> Is rounded with a sleep."
>
> *Shakespeare,* " The Tempest," IV. i.

" DREAMS are witnessed," says R. L. Stevenson,* " in that small theatre of the brain which we keep brightly lighted all night long, after the jets are down, and darkness and sleep reign undisturbed in the remainder of the body." They are little plays in which we are actors, with an audience of one; they are fantastic and romantic, tragic and comic, with " Fears and tortures, and the touch of joy."† Through thousands of years they have come and gone, as regular as sleep, always preserving their mystery, and defying scientific analysis to this very day. It is our purpose in this book to see in what manner they have been esteemed and interpreted by barbarian and cultured nations, blacks and whites, now and in the past. We would know how man, in all his stages

*" Across the Plains."   †Byron, " The Dream," Stanza I

from the brute, has looked upon this startling phenomenon, seeing that at the present day he is on the verge of solving the long msytery.

Dreams are hallucinations, and sometimes even delusions. Hallucinations, or the creation of something imaginary out of nothing real, a characteristic of powerful states of excitement and certain forms of insanity, are not so common in human experience as illusions, a mistaking one thing for another, as when the sun appears to move across the sky, when really it does nothing of the kind, the motion being mistakenly associated with the object.

Hallucinations, however, are not infrequent, even in the persistent form of delusions. Lunatics think they are Queen Victoria or Napoleon — a delusion; a peritonitis patient complains that a church congress is sitting inside her, and she can hear the speakers' voices — a hallucination; people afflicted with *paranoia hallucinatoria* hear taunting voices repeating their thoughts and following them about the streets; and other deranged people think they entertain, in daylight and wide-awake, kings, princesses, and angels. Blake, the artist and poet, was punished by his father for telling lies when he declared, honestly enough from his point of view, that he was late for tea because he had been delayed by " *Ezekiel* sitting under a green bough," and " a tree full of angels at Peckham." Hysterical people and others dream of black cats, snakes and similar creatures; it used to be thought, indeed, that they were fast in league with the devil; and often enough, so absolute are their delusions, they have confessed to secret practices and endured the rack, the ducking stool and the stake rather than deny them.

Hallucinations are extraordinarily vivid, taking the reason by storm and compelling at least a momentary belief in their reality. Ordinary dreaming affects us like ordinary life, and for the time being imposes upon us. Wundt even calls it a state of "normal temporary insanity"; and this has been accepted before today as a valid plea in a murder trial. An inveterate somnambulist in the middle of the night, fancying the child sleeping beside him was a wild beast about to spring, picked it up in a frenzy of fear, and dashed its brains out against the wall. He was horrified when he realized his mistake; but he was tried on a charge of wilful murder. The court, however, holding the opinion that a man could not be responsible for a crime done in his sleep, he was acquitted.*

Dreams are more often than not visual. You may seem to speak, and quite understand what

* Reported by Dr. Clouston of Edinburgh; see Chambers' Encyclopædia, Vol. IV, 1901, art. " Dreaming."

others seem to say, without the issue of **any** audible sound; a sort of intuition tells you. Doors may shut hard, and rifles fire, without sounds being heard, and yet they seem natural enough as long as the dream lasts.

All the same, sounds *are* heard in dreams; and it is not uncommon to experience also smells and tastes.

Experiments have been performed to find out the percentage of dreams relating to each of the senses, and the investigators, while naturally differing in detail, agree in the general conclusion that there are about seven sight dreams to three of hearing, the remaining sense-dreams being almost negligible. Prof. W. S. Monroe's analysis, after an examination of three hundred dreams of fifty-five of the women students of Westfield Normal School, Massachusetts, was as follows:

Taste impressions in fewer than 1 per cent of the dreams;

Smell impressions in rather more than 1 per cent;

Movement impressions in 5 per cent;

Touch impressions in 3 per cent;

Hearing impressions in 26 per cent; and

Sight impressions in 67 per cent.

Professor Monroe then followed up this experiment by another, to determine how far dreams of any particular sort could be stimulated intentionally; and he tried to procure taste dreams.

Twenty students were chosen, a crushed clove was put on each one's tongue before she fell asleep, the dreams were reported next day, and the process was repeated twenty times. There were two hundred and fifty dreams reported, but only in seventeen were there taste impressions (and only three were of cloves); in short, impressions just before sleep by no means always produce similar impressions in dreams and taste dreams least of all.

Dreams are not singular only in preferring one of the senses to the others; they also depart from the normal appearance and order of things in daily life, and violate the dreamer's moral principles. One Napier, a man who was kindness itself, dreamed, for example, that when he encountered his best friend, he ran him through the body with his sword,* thoroughly enjoying the sensation, and feeling a thrill of pleasure to see the point of the sword issue from his friend's back. Napier could not have dreamed such a thing, if his moral sense had been as alive and as strong as in his waking hours; his conscience was either too feeble to act, or else in total abeyance.

The same fate appears to overtake the sense of proportion and humor in dreams, or we should never tolerate the absurdities of transposition and caricature that we do.

* See article by Miss Cobbe, Macmillan's Magazine, 1873.

" Many monstrous forms in sleep we see,
   That neither were, nor are, nor e'er can be."

But while the dream lasts, they hold good, in a sort of land where " whatever is, is right." For a non-swimmer to swim, and a blind man to see, and a cripple to fly, are merely normal occurrences in dreams.

Paralysis is a favorite dream infliction of unparalytic people; a lion is going to spring, but they are rooted to the spot —

"My spirits, as in a dream, are all bound up "; however, the lion is similarly paralyzed, and the sequel is less disastrous than anticipated. Indeed inconsistencies and extravagances are hardly ever absent from dreams.

Of the first of these there is a typical example in Hood's " Whims and Oddities." It " occurred when I was on the eve of marriage, a season when, if lovers sleep sparingly they dream profusely. A brief slumber sufficed to carry me in the night coach to Bognor. It had been concerted between Honoria and myself that we should pass the honeymoon at some place along the coast.

"The purpose of my solitary journey was to procure an appropriate dwelling, which, we had agreed upon, should be a little pleasant house, with an indispensable lookout upon the sea. I chose one accordingly, a pretty villa, with bow-windows, and a prospect delightfully marine. The ocean murmur sounded incessantly upon the beach. A decent elderly body, in decayed sables, undertook on her part to promote the comfort of the occupants by every suitable attention and, as she assured me, at a very reasonable rate. So far the nocturnal faculty had served me truly. A daydream could not have proceeded more orderly. But, alas! just here, when the dwelling was selected, the sea view was secured, the rent agreed upon, when everything was plausible, consistent and rational, the incoherent fancy crept in, and confounded all — by marrying me to the old woman of the house! "

Robert MacNish gave two elaborate examples of similar dreams in his pioneer work, " The Philosophy of Sleep," published in 1834. He said after reading Hoffman's " The Devil's Elixir ", " I dreamed that I possessed ubiquity, twenty resemblances of myself appearing in as many different places, in the same room and each being so thoroughly possessed by my own mind that I could not ascertain which of them was myself, and which my double, etc. On this occasion, fancy travelled so far into the regions of absurdity that I conceived myself riding upon my own back — one of the resemblances being mounted upon another, and both animated with the soul appertaining to myself, in such a manner that I knew not whether I was the carrier or the carried."

And another time, while he was interested in heathen mythology, he had this dream: "I was converted into a mighty pillar of stone, which reared its head in the midst of a desert, where it stood for ages, till generation after generation melted away before it. Even in this state, though unconscious of possessing any organs of sense, or being else than a mass of lifeless stone, I saw every object around — the mountains growing bald with age, the forest trees drooping in decay. At last, I waxed old and began to crumble into dust, while the moss and ivy accumulated upon me and stamped me with the aspect of hoar antiquity."

A dream like this will seem to last a lifetime, though its real length may be but a moment. An oft-told dream, illustrating this extraordinary time-perspective, is contained in an old handbook on dreams. At the first stroke of midnight by the parish-clock, a certain man fell asleep, and dreamed a dream. He ran away to sea, served on board ship for a long time, and, just escaping with his life from a shipwreck, swam to a desert island. No rescue arriving he began to abandon hope, when at last a ship hove in sight and took him on board. He became a ringleader in a successful mutiny, took charge of the ship himself, and sailed it across remote and uncharted seas. At length wearying of this life, he sailed for

England, sold the ship and entered business on shore.

One day, some one recognized him as a mutineer; he was arrested and tried, condemned to death and led off to execution; but at the eleventh hour, when the noose was round his neck, and he was expecting death at any moment, he awoke with a start, and heard — the last of the twelve strokes of the clock.

Nor need this be a fiction, and exaggerated; drowning men, it is said, in their last moments see all the events of their lifetime pass before their eyes in a swift vision. De Quincey said his opium dreams seemed to stretch out to seventy or a hundred years; so that, to judge from *within* the mind, " Rip Van Winkle," and " The Sleeping Beauty," are mere common sense. Yet dreams, doubtless, take a very short time in actual enactment, though not necessarily only an instant; dogs may be seen indeed, by their yelps and convulsive starts, to dream for many minutes.

Other creatures, cats, sheep, cows, horses, monkeys, parrots and the like dream, too. " You will see horses when their limbs shall be stretched in sleep, yet perpetually perspiring and panting, and apparently exerting their utmost strength for the palm of victory, or often starting in their sleep as if the barriers were just set open."*

* Lucretius, " De Rerum Naturae."

" Nightingales dream, and a nightingale-dream at that, for you can hear them chirping very softly and singing very low." *

But dogs are the best known of non-human dreamers. They seem to accompany their dreams by mimic actions, jerking out their legs, twitching their ears, breathing hard, and uttering sharp cries. " Oftentimes, after they are awakened, they still follow in imagination the empty images of stags, as if they saw them turned to flight; until, their hallucinations being dispelled, they return to their senses.† It is a favorite observation in poetry. " The staghounds," sang Sir Walter Scott,

> " weary with the chase,
> Lay stretch'd upon the rushy floor,
> And urged in dreams the forest race,
> From Teviot-stone to Eskdale Moor."

The contents of our dreams, unlike the above, are not generally easy to connect with our experience; many are so fantastic that the dreamer will utterly deny having conceived of such things before. This all adds to the mystery and charm; and so, though many authorities have declared that nothing is seen in dreams that has not been seen or conceived of awake, the mass of mankind have never been persuaded of its truth. The difficulty and the mystery have this phenomenon superadded — that there is a powerful tendency

* Buffon, " Birds," IX Vol., p. 151.
† " De Rerum Naturae," Lucretius.

to forget dreams; most are certainly altogether obliterated next day, and those that remain are rarely remembered in accurate detail.

If the same things happened to us awake as frequently happen in our dreams, we should remember them in every particular to our dying day; but the dream life is somehow apart from the main current of our existence, and affects it in a relatively small degree. It not infrequently happens that in a dream we are conscious of having been in the same place in some previous dream, though we do not perhaps remember it next day, and cannot identify it as an objective reality; it is as if the dream life had a partial continuity of its own, parallel to that of waking life, with a possibility of regularly inhabiting a certain dream dwelling, night after night, or on occasions separated by an interval of years.

The acted dream, peculiar to sleep walkers, is forgotten as readily as the imaginary, though the dexterity displayed, as in performing feats of balance and of strength, may be comparable to that of waking life. When Angel Clare, on strained terms with his wife Tess on their honeymoon,* walked into her room in his sleep, and bore her out of the house in his arms, crying, " Dead! dead! dead! " and " My poor, poor Tess — my dearest darling Tess! So sweet, so good, so true! " he

* " Tess of the D'Urbervilles," Chapter 36.

carried "her over a bridge that it was a feat of balancing to traverse, he took her up to the ruined choir of the abbey-church . . . his whole proceeding so far being a repetition of his action, some months before of bodily carrying Marian, Izzy, and Tess through the flooded fields. In the choir there stood a stone coffin, into which Angel sat Tess, himself lying down on the ground alongside." When directed by her to go back he picked her up again and carried her back to her room. Then as a child will cry or talk or beat his fists in sleep, and not know anything about it afterwards, so it was with Angel, who, to the bitter disappointment of Tess, showed no recollection whatever next morning of the incident so fresh and green in her memory.

Waking dreams are as illusory, but not as common, as sleeping ones; and they often lead to the assumption of a supernatural visitation.

If one reflects how many ghosts and other miraculous apparitions are seen at night, and when the mind is in a more or less somnolent condition, the idea is forcibly suggested that a good proportion of these visions are the *debris* of dreams. In some cases indeed, as that of Spinoza, the hallucination (of a "scurvy black Brazilian") is recognized by the subject himself as a dream image. I am indebted to Mr. W. H. Pollock for a fact which curiously illustrates the position here adopted. A lady was staying at a country house. During the night and immediately on waking up she had an apparition of a strange-looking man in mediæval costume, a figure by no means agreeable, which seemed altogether unfamiliar to her.

" The next morning on rising she recognized the original of her hallucinatory image in a portrait hanging on the wall of her bedroom, which must have impressed itself on her brain before the occurrence of the apparition, though she had not attended to it. Oddly enough, she now learned for the first time that the house at which she was staying had the reputation of being haunted, and by the very same somewhat repulsive-looking mediæval personage that had troubled her intersomnolent moments. The case seems to me to be typical with respect to the genesis of ghosts, and of the reputation of haunted houses.''*

However, we need to beware of too materialistic a notion of ghosts, and dreams, too. There is a form of illusion that makes us think mere change of point of view is progress of thought; it may really be that men were saner in the days when they believed in ghosts and super-natural dreams than today when they discredit the former, and regard the latter as compensatory hallucinations preserving the balance of the nervous system.

If by explaining dreams scientifically we ex-

* Sully's " Illusions — A Psychological Study." 1905.

plained away all their romance, the progress we
lay claim to would be doubtful.

> " Great God! I'd rather be
> A Pagan suckled in a creed outworn,—
> So might I, standing on this pleasant lea,
> Have glimpses that would make me less forlorn;
> Have sight of Proteus rising from the sea;
> Or hear old Triton blow his wreathéd horn."

We need to guard ourselves at the outset from
any disdain of outworn ideas and primitive faiths,
and to read the story of what dreams have been
to man as a poetical and, in essence, a sacred
record. Dreams fulfilled their function five thousand years ago no less well than they fulfil them
today. It is only the " trappings and the suits "
that have changed with the process of time.

CHAPTER II

DREAMS AS REALITIES

" Our life is twofold: Sleep hath its own world,
A boundary between the things misnamed
Death and existence: Sleep hath its own world,
And a wide realm of wild reality."
                    Byron, " The Dream."

A TRIBE of Arizona Red Indians taking part in his film picture " Molly Coddle," Mr. Douglas Fairbanks thought that they might enjoy seeing themselves on the screen afterwards, and so gave them a private exhibition. However, some of the Indians having died meanwhile, when the remainder saw a war-dance on the screen, with the dead men taking part, they rose up as one man and fled from the enclosure, exclaiming that they had seen ghosts.

Incidents similar in substance to this happen often enough, however, in our own life. The staircase from the hair-cutting saloon to the flat above, in a certain barber's shop in London, forms a bend about halfway up, where a tall looking-glass is fixed against the wall. Not long after the installation of the glass, Spider, the cat, came bounding downstairs, and reached the corner, but seeing another cat bounding alongside, tried to stop short. He was going so fast that he reached the saloon floor before he could turn round, but he sprang upstairs again to the corner, and darted head first at the other cat, which seemed also to have sprung upstairs, and with the same intention. Spider hurt his nose pretty badly, with repeated blows at the looking-glass, before he realized the futility of the attempt, and gave it up as a bad job. The other cat drawing back at the same time, Spider retreated, without in the slightest degree realizing, however, that there is a difference between a cat in the flesh and a cat in a looking-glass. Primitive man, we must needs suppose, is in the position of Spider.

One wall of the hair-cutting saloon, too, was a looking-glass; and on the day of Spider's encounter, a naval man brought into the shop his three-year-old son, in a sailor suit, and set him down on the floor to amuse himself, while waiting his turn. Then the little boy (we shall call him Jack), noticing another little fellow, also in a sailor suit, at the other side of the room, at once ran forward to make friends with him, while the other boy made a corresponding movement. To avoid colliding, Jack turned and took two steps to the right, but his new-found friend's doing the same still endangered him, and so he took a quick turn to the left, which again his double followed.

Impatient and nonplussed, Jack now turned round, and saw the customers laughing at him; and, at length, he fell to suspecting the deceit. There *was* no other little Jack; it was only the looking-glass beguiling him. Up to now Jack had been in the Red Indian stage, but this lesson was teaching him to distinguish images from realities; and so to climb another rung of sophistication. He was outgrowing the poetry and faith of the savage, and acquiring the reason and subtlety of civilized man.

Man's earliest conception of dreams is just this literal belief; what appears before him in dreams is as real as what appears before him awake, and the people of his dream stand veritably before him. A Red Indian (untouched by white influences, that is), dreaming of his dead parents, believes he sees their souls, and has communication in very fact with the dead; whereas a civilized European would think it was an unconscious brain adjustment, or, more likely, the ill effects of supper. A savage, seeing his reflection in the water, thinks it is his soul, which a water spirit may seize at any moment; a civilized man would say it was the reflection of rays of light, with the angle of incidence equal to the angle of reflection. Probably we are nearer the scientific truth; we are certainly prosier.

The Greenlander hunts, fishes and woos as

much in his dreams as awake. The Dyaks of
Borneo travel where they will in their dreams,
and welcome their friends as visitors; but should
they dream of falling into a stream, next morning
on awaking they send for a wizard to fish for their
souls with a hand net in a basin of water, and so
restore them.

" One morning," writes Im Thurm, in " Among
the Indians in Guiana," " when it was important
to me to get away from a camp on the Essequibo
River, at which I had been detained for some
days by the illness of some of my Indian com-
panions, I found that one of the invalids, a young
Macusi, though better in health, was so enraged
against me that he refused to stir, for he declared
that, with great want of consideration for his
weak health, I had taken him out during the
night and had made him haul the canoe up a
series of difficult cataracts. Nothing could persuade him that this was but a dream, and it was
some time before he was so far pacified as to
throw himself sulkily into the bottom of the canoe.
At that time we were all suffering from a great
scarcity of food, and hunger having its usual
effect in producing vivid dreams, similar events
frequently occurred. More than once the men
declared in the morning that some absent man,
whom they named, had come during the night,
and had beaten, or otherwise maltreated them;

and they insisted on much rubbing of the bruised part of their bodies."

To the Zulu the appearance of one of his ancestors in his dreams is a sign of impending disaster, the " itongo " having come from the next life to give him a warning; or if the man is absent from his tribe, the disaster threatens them, and it is his duty to go and warn them.

The Indians on the other hand hold a different notion; and when an old squaw in British Columbia dreamed nightly of her ancestors, she sent for the medicine man to exorcise them, as they plagued her in her sleep.

A further reason with some races for fearing the souls of the dead is the belief that a departed soul can command a sleeper to go along with it on the lone path to the land of spirits, and the sleeper dies. Thus, for fear that the deceased's soul may be lurking in the neighborhood, the Aru Islanders will not sleep in a house where a death has recently taken place, and the mourners at a funeral among the Upper Thompson Indians will not stay in the house of the deceased.

This attitude towards dreams, of accepting them literally as realities, is probably one held by all races in the early stages of their development; not that they hold any theory in a conscious way, but that they respond directly to their dreams, as to the other phenomena of nature, and do not distinguish dream perceptions from waking. No doubt they pay little heed to most of their dreams, as we do, but take the vivid and startling ones very much to heart; their dreams are a continuation of waking life, with equal possibilities of friendship, love and war. " The dead relations and friends," writes Mr. Edward Clodd, " who appear in dreams and live their old life, with whom he joins in the battle, the chase, and the feast, the foes with whom he struggles, the wild beasts from whom he flies, or in whose clutches he feels himself, and with shrieks awakens his squaw, the long distances he travels to summer climes lit by a light that never was on land or sea, are all 'real,' and no 'baseless fabric of a vision.' That now and again he should have walked in his sleep would confirm the seeming reality; still more so would the intensified form of dreaming called ' nightmare,' when hideous spectres sit upon the breast stopping breath and paralyzing motion, and to which is largely due the creation of a vast army of nocturnal demons that fill the folklore of the world, and that, under infinite variety of repellent forms, have had place in the hierarchy of religions."[*]

The world of the dream believer is thus larger than our unbelievers' world, by the size of his dreams; there are " darker woods and stranger

* " Myth and Dreams," 1891.

hills; brighter skies, more dangerous waters; sweeter flowers, more tempting fruits; wider plains, drearier deserts, sunnier fields. . . . As to our sun, it is a burning heaven —the world of gods."*

It is at this stage that man realizes, as much from these dream experiences as from any other observations, that he is not just a body, but first a spiritual being; he has a soul. Echoes support this animistic theory; they are held, for example, by the Sonora Indians, to be the voices of the departed, who dwell in caves and in the hollows of cliffs. Shadows, too, are soul evidences. The strange voices, the yet stranger appearances in dreams, confirm the supposition that in each man, and in each of the phenomena of nature, dwells a soul possessing transcendent powers. And though this primitive animism dies out as the race rises in culture, the most highly civilized peoples are prone to the same belief in another form — and it was never so popular as it is today — namely, spiritualism; " the cultural conditions are altogether different, yet the mental attitude recurs."†

Expression is bounded by, and bound up with, experience; and the differentiation of an image from a reality being long in obtaining verbal

* Charlotte Brontë.
† " Psychology and Folk Lore," page 82, by R. R. Marett, M.A., D.Sc., 1920.

form, difficulty of expression in words adds to the difficulty of apprehension of the idea. How can Jack, the sailor boy, acquaint a companion with his discovery of his mirror self, if he has not heard the words " reflection " or " image "? And these are not simple words for him; he is on terms of intimacy with " boy " rather than with " my reflection," and he could be expected to give a companion no better an account of his experience than that he had seen at the barber's shop a boy in appearance like himself, and carrying out the same actions — only he was in a glass! This would neither convey the whole truth, nor prevent his companion from calling him a deliberate story-teller.

From such a course, the El Gran Chaco Indians are reputed great liars; their talent for telling tall stories — for the truth of which they are ready to vouch — is undoubtedly due to dreams and the lack of words to express the difference between their waking feats and others. This is no isolated example. A Baroro village was thrown into a panic and deserted on the report of a villager that he had seen an enemy advance guard closing in upon them; when the expected attack did not take place, the villagers returned, and ultimately found out that the timorous villager had only dreamed it!

London school children are similarly hazy at

distinguishing dream phenomena; and the few children that really can are able to give only garbled accounts of their dreams, on account of their poor vocabulary and inexactitude — indeed they frequently convey the very opposite meaning to what they intend.* Our adult power of distinction is acquired, not innate, and is comparable to our power of reading and computing.

Dream beings are thus, in the early stages of culture, considered people's souls; and indeed this helps to give rise to man's conception of himself. The powers the soul is credited with vary, therefore, with the conception of dreams held by the race. Thus the American Indians limit the soul's activities to the people and haunts that in the waking state it loves and desires to see; in Chaucer's words —

> " The wery hunter, slepinge in his bed,
>   To wode ayein his minde goth anoon;
>   The juge dremeth how his plees been sped;
>   The carter dremeth how his cartes goon:
>   The riche, of golde; the knight fight with his foon,
>   The sicke met† he drinketh of the tonne;
>   The lover met he hath his lady wonne."‡

Other races allow the soul more freedom and power. As for the sequel next day, the Indians say that the dreamer must try and obtain the

---

* See the Report of Dr. C. W. Kimmins, Chief Inspector to the London Education Committee, in an address to the Child Study Society, February, 1919.

† The sick man dreams.

‡ " The Parlement of Foules."

things dreamed of, for neglect of which his soul may be troubled both now and in the hereafter.

A limitation fixed by the Karens shows that they have observed how the scenery of dreams is derived from that of waking experience; for they say that the soul cannot frequent a place unless it has been previously visited in reality. On the other hand the Maoris impose no geographical limits; and so constantly does the soul travel according to the Indians of Guiana that one may say a man sleeps or wakes according to whether his soul is abroad or in the body; waking up is the sign of the soul's return — and on no account must that be interfered with, if the sleeping person does not want to die.

This is the origin of curious customs, regulations and beliefs among certain races. It is a crime for a member of the Miningkabauen tribe of Sumatra to stain or blacken the face of any sleeping person, because it would disguise the sleeper and confuse the returning soul. The Patani Malays say that the errant soul will not come back to a painted sleeper until the paint is washed off; and there are sects in Bombay that punish those that tamper with a sleeper's looks as for murder. The Tajals of the Luzon Islands prohibit, on pain of heavy punishment, the awakening of a sleeping person, lest his soul be so far off that it has not time to return before the body is assumed to be dead; and other tribes order awakening to be gradual and gentle, and declare that the soul's entry may be detected by a sneeze.

It is supposed that sometimes, in spite of the precautions taken, a soul will enter the wrong body, by mistake or in revenge, and the person will then be afflicted with a disease: he is possessed of a devil. The expulsion of the alien spirit is undertaken by a medicine man, who tries exorcism, noise, pinching, and other similar measures. An old Dakota, consulting a medicine man about his son's sore eyes, explained to him that his son, some thirty years before, as a boy had stuck a pin in the end of a stick, and speared a minnow with it. "Isn't it strange," he ended up, "that after such a lapse of time the spirit of the fish should come for revenge?" The medicine man then resorted to incantations and grimaces to drive the minnow's spirit out; and also tried other recognized methods of treatment, such as yells, the beating of drums, and clashing of cymbals, which no doubt were intended to drown the patient's groans as well as effect a cure. These did not succeed, and he was forced to try starving and beating the patient, which was eventually an effective cure.

When Iron Arms, a great Redskin warrior, died in his bed in time of peace, his death was announced to be the result of a medicine man's mistake, in having treated him for possession by the soul of a prairie-dog when the true cause was the soul of a mud-hen. On the other hand, there are races that consider it no disgrace for a warrior to die in his bed, because his soul may have met with some enemy in a dream and have been defeated by it in battle; for it would be debarred from returning to the body, whereas, had it won, he would have enjoyed the glow of victory all the next day.

The Choctaw Indians believe that each man has two spirits, the external one (or shadow), and the internal — the " shilombish " and the " shilup "; but only the latter survives after bodily death. The Fijians call the shadow the " dark spirit," which at death goes to the unseen world; but the " light spirit," or reflection in water, remains eternally to haunt the spot where the death has taken place.

The place of exit and entry for the soul, on its nocturnal excursions from the body, has been settled in various ways in different countries. An old German belief held that it was the mouth, the soul taking the form of a little bird or white mouse, and having the power to go out or return only when the mouth was open; and in Transylvania children used to be warned never to sleep with the mouth open, for fear the soul should slip out like a mouse and abandon the child, who would die. Other places of egress and entry have also had a following.

Nor are these fantastic conceptions without relationship to civilized theories; the theory of Democritus (fifth century B. C.) indeed is very similar. This regarded bodies as a host of atoms in a state of constant agitation, casting a sort of shadow or image of their total bulk in streams of finer particles; and under special circumstances, such as sleep, the shadows might become visible, and we should see as it were the soul of the object, or a nebula of the same shape. A dream would then be a reality.

However that may be, the human instinct is to attach to dreams the significance of reality. It is man's first reading of the phenomenon — and sometimes his last. What, then, is the effect of this belief on religious ideas? To what conception of man's spiritual self does it lead?

Man has an individual soul (at first thought solid, but later ethereal), distinct and separate from the body, yet mysteriously related to it; and, as in sleep we observe, possessed of supernatural powers, by means of which it can transcend the ordinary limitations of time and space. This soul, as shadows, reflections, and dreams all bear witness, resembles the body to which it belongs, in its shape and appearance. Life, therefore, is not purely practical and material, but surpasses waking thought, being in fact an awe-inspiring mystery. Stocks and stones, animals and birds and human beings all possess souls, which may exercise an influence for good or for evil, and must be worshipped or propitiated according to their moods, which are known to medicine men.

Religion of this kind, polytheism, is not a matter of expediency or intellectual acceptance, but of deep-rooted conviction founded on daily personal experience. It is a natural religion, satisfying the needs of men at a certain stage in their evolution, and preparing the way for the great revealed religions of the world. The gods and heroes of Greece are the precursors of the saints, apostles, angels, and deities of a religion of deeper insight into existence.

Dreams are thus in large part the fashioners of early religions, and so they wield a powerful influence on the great religions, too:

> " they become
> A portion of ourselves as of our time,
> And look like heralds of eternity."

CHAPTER III

DREAMS AS VISIONS

" They speak
Like sibyls of the future." — *Byron.*

" Where, I pray, ye Trojan dames, can I behold the divine spirit of
Helenus, or Cassandra, that they may interpret my dreams? For I
beheld a dappled hind torn by the blood-stained fang of the wolf,
forcibly dragged from my bosom, a miserable sight."

Euripides, " Hecuba."

TODAY, man is curious about and credulous of
the supernatural, and he has always been so; for
belief in the supernatural means faith in the con-
tinual possibility of miracle and romance, of com-
munion with the loved dead, and the righting of
all wrongs. The materialist has dried up a source
of knowledge, power and joy; and often enough
nature wreaks her revenge by transforming the
middle-aged dogmatic scientist into the old-aged
convinced spiritualist. Ages of materialism, like
our own, contain the seeds of their own destruction, in growing religious movements that, however foolish and sophistical, augment their numbers
of adherents day by day. Man asks, why *should*
life come to an abrupt stop, with the merely
material round and common task? Why should
the living, so mysteriously born, remain utterly

separated from the dead, so mysteriously taken
away?

> " To die, — to sleep; —
> To sleep! perchance to dream?"

Dante has portrayed that farther life, which
we would fain know for ourselves, and bear witness
of to others; and dreams are the likeliest of all
avenues to it —

> " Some say that gleams of a remoter world
> Visit the soul in sleep."*

It is an old belief, and long cherished. " For
God speaketh once, yea twice, yet man perceiveth
it not. In a dream, in a vision of the night, when
deep sleep falleth upon men, in slumbering upon
the bed; then he openeth the ears of men, and
sealeth their instruction." Thus the Jews believed
in direct messages from God in dreams. On one
occasion, " God came to Abimelech in a dream
by night, and said to him, Behold, Thou art but
a dead man, for the woman which thou hast
taken; for she is a man's wife."† Angels are the
chosen messengers; and so when Jacob dreamed,
" behold a ladder set up on earth, and the top
of it reached to heaven: and behold the angels of
God ascending and descending upon it. And
behold the Lord stood above it, and said, I am
the Lord God of Abraham thy father, and the

* Shelley, " Mont Blanc."
† Genesis, Chap. 20.

God of Isaac: the land whereon thou liest, to thee will I give it, and to thy seed."* And again, " the angel of God spake unto me in a dream, saying, Jacob: And I said, Here am I. And he said . . . I am the God of Beth-el . . . now arise, get thee out from this land, and return unto the land of thy kindred."†

These dreams are plain messages requiring no interpretation. There are other examples, too, for " in Gibeon the Lord appeared to Solomon in a dream by night: and God said, Ask what I shall give thee;"‡ and " Behold, the angel of the Lord appeared unto him (Joseph, the father of Jesus) in a dream, saying, Joseph, thou son of David, fear not to take unto thee Mary thy wife: for that which is conceived in her is of the Holy Ghost." " The Lord stood by him (St. Paul), and said, Be of good cheer, Paul: for as thou hast testified of me in Jerusalem, so must thou bear witness also at Rome;"§ and again later, "There stood by me this night the angel of God, whose I am, and whom I serve, saying, Fear not Paul; thou must be brought before Caesar: and, lo, God has given thee all them that sail with thee."

But on other occasions, and in order, amongst other reasons, to render the message memorable the dream was not clear on the face of it, but

‡ Genesis, Chap. 29. § Ibid, Chap. 31.
* I Kings, Chap. 3.
† St. Matthew, Chap. 1. Acts, Chap. 23.

consisted of a symbolical dumb show, which conveyed no meaning but to the initiated, and yet which impelled the dreamer, by its vividness, to realize the divine origin of his vision — like Joseph's.

" And Joseph dreamed a dream, and he told it to his brethren: and they hated him yet the more. And he said unto them, Hear, I pray you, this dream which I have dreamed. For, behold, we were binding sheaves in the field, and lo, my sheaf arose, and also stood upright; and behold, your sheaves stood round about, and made obeisance to my sheaf. And his brethren said to him, Shalt thou indeed reign over us? or shalt thou indeed have dominion over us? And they hated him yet the more for his dreams, and for his words. And he dreamed yet another dream, and told it to his brethren, and said, Behold I have dreamed a dream more; and, behold, the sun and the moon and the eleven stars made obeisance to me. And he told it to his father, and to his brethren: and his father rebuked him, and said unto him, what is this dream which thou hast dreamed? Shall I and thy mother and thy brethren indeed come to bow down ourselves to thee to the earth? "

The symbolism here is simple, and, the circumstances of the occasion being known, it was easy to decipher it; but numbers of other dreams were not so easily interpreted; and so the custom

arose of maintaining seers about the royal courts.
Ordinary dreams went unregarded, as with ourselves, but vivid ones, particularly if they occurred
more than once, were accredited to supernatural
interposition; and it was then that the skill of the
interpreter was called in to aid in reading the
message. The Jewish interpreters read a symbolic
meaning into the images seen, but unlike their
neighbors they used no incantations, or astrology,
or occult science.

The dreams of Pharaoh's butler and baker
were interpreted thus by their symbols. " And
they said unto him (Joseph), We have dreamed
a dream, and there is no interpreter of it. And
Joseph said unto them, Do not interpretations
belong to God? Tell me them, I pray you. And
the chief butler told his dream to Joseph, and
said to him, In my dream, behold a vine was
before me; And in the vine were three branches:
and it was as though it budded, and her blossoms
shot forth; and the clusters thereof brought forth
ripe grapes, and I pressed them into Pharaoh's
cup, and I gave the cup into Pharaoh's hand.
And Joseph said unto him, This is the interpretation of it: The three branches are three days:
Yet within three days shall Pharaoh lift up thine
head, and restore thee unto thy place: and thou
shalt deliver Pharaoh's cup into his hand, after
the former manner when thou wast his butler.

When the chief baker saw that the interpretation was good, he said unto Joseph, I also was in my dream, and, behold had three white baskets on my head: And in the uppermost basket there was of all manner of bakemeats for Pharaoh: and the birds did eat them out of the basket upon my head. And Joseph answered and said, This is the interpretation thereof: The three baskets are three days. Yet within three days shall Pharaoh lift up thy head from off thee, and shall hang thee on a tree; and the birds shall eat thy flesh from off thee."

These interpretations are rather less obvious than the last; they are also of a different sort of dream. Joseph's had been from God: but it is hardly likely that the release and the expiation respectively of the butler and the baker would be the object of divine interposition; these dreams were no doubt of the kind interpreted in dream books, namely, arbitrary foretellers of future events. However, even of these Joseph claims that God is the interpreter.

That Pharaoh's dreams were of divine origin is implied from the text; and they were hard problems in interpretation. The seven good kine stood for seven years of great plenty, the seven lean kine for seven years of famine; " And for that the dream was doubled unto Pharaoh twice; it is because the thing is established by God and

God will shortly bring it to pass." Nebuchadnezzar* and Daniel† had similar dreams; and Gideon‡ heard one such interpreted.

The Jews, at various times, thus held more than one conception of the function of dreams: they were direct messages from God, Himself or His angels pronouncing them; or they were symbolic pictures, sometimes obvious in meaning, at others only to be explained by accredited interpreters, who were instructed, not by a dream book (as among the Arabs), but by the wisdom of God; or they were revelations from God, obtainable by solicitation, which would sometimes be unavailing — " God is departed from me," said Saul, " and answereth me no more, neither by prophets nor by dreams."§ This is all an advance on the primitive realism of man's first stages in that only certain dreams, visions of a special memorableness, bear a supernatural meaning, and they generally require subtle interpretation.

Among the Israelites, as among other peoples at a similar stage, it was common to regard a man of frequent visions as a chosen vessel for divine communications — he is, as the Zulus say, a " house of dreams "; however the great prophets challenged this tendency, and Jeremiah was enjoined not to hearken " to your prophets, nor

* Daniel, Chap. IV, II.   † Daniel, Chap. VII, VIII.
‡ Judges, Chap. VII, v. 14.
§ I Samuel, Chap. XXVIII, v. 5.

to your diviners, nor to your *dreamers*, nor to your enchanters, nor to your sorcerers, which speak unto you saying, Ye shall not serve the King of Babylon."

In Syria, Babylonia and Egypt, dreams composed a regular division of the system of divination; and its importance may be judged by the many dreams recorded on extant monuments in Egypt. The interpreters, who were officers of the court, were called " Masters of the Secret Things," and sometimes " The Learned Men of the Magic Library." The recorded dreams are typically direct, some are unsolicited, the gods appearing and demanding an act of piety towards themselves, or administering a warning; and others are solicited, the gods granting the worshippers an answer to a definite question.* Dreams were thus considered essentially real and unsymbolic, yet there is an advance on the simple travel realism described in the last chapter, the outcome of an unconsciously held theory of the hypersensitiveness of sleep, by which the sleeper can see and hear divine beings that are indeed always present but are too ethereal for the gross waking senses. Sleep induces a sort of ecstasy, and dreams are the functioning of a lucid hypersensitiveness induced by it.

---

* See Hastings' " Encyclopædia of Religion and Ethics," Article on " Dreams and Sleep," for much interesting detail.

Probably not at court, but certainly among the common people, magic was practised, and jingles of words were chanted to induce dreams, or accord interpretations. The magicians made lavish use of the popular awe inspired by the ghosts of the dead in dreams. " The well-known Leyden papyrus is the type *par excellence* of cases of a dead woman coming to torment her husband in dreams. The way to get rid of this torment was to make a statuette of the dead wife and tie upon its wrist a list of the husband's good deeds during his wedded life, and then a summons to the ghost to stop her persecution, under the threat of proceedings before the god of the dead."*

In later times additions were made to the number of kinds of spirits that could appear, the magicians adding those of suicides, executed criminals (the germ of the idea of demons), and ill-disposed gods; and with ceremonial developments, of incantations, fastings, ritual, drug-taking, the path was prepared that led to the black magic of Mediterranean countries.

In Greece, too, dreams were considered channels of intercourse with supernatural powers. As in the Bible God sent the dreams by angels, so in Homer Zeus sent dreams by Mercury. Actual persons seemed to stand before the dreamer, and speak to him; and these were personated by a

* Hastings' " Encyclopædia of Religion and Ethics."

tribe of " shades," a " people of dreams " dwelling " on the dim path to the land of the dead,"* who, when summoned, assumed the form of the person intended, presented themselves at the head of the sleeper on his couch, and pronounced their message as they were instructed. However, as Jove was the god of the overlords, it was only their dreams that were to be considered divine, those of other men being of no account unless some recognized interpreter of dreams said they were exceptions.

The Greek idea may be considered broadly, in the words of one of their poets, as reducing to this, that

> " Dreams are in general reflex images
> Of things that men in waking hours have known;
> But sometimes dreams of loftier character
> Rise in the tranced soul, inspired by Jove,
> Prophetic of the future." †

Of the working of the machinery there are innumerable examples in Greek literature.

When Minerva, Ulysses being then hard by his long-sought home, wished to inspire Penelope to resist the importunate suitors to the last, she sent her a dream by one of the shades. " Sleep's gentle powers " having invaded Penelope's drooping eyes,

* Odyssey, XXIV, 12.
† Aceius

> " Minerva, life-like, on embodied air
> Impress'd the form of Iphthima the fair. . .
> As Pallas will'd, along the sable skies
> To calm the queen, the phantom-sister flies.
> Swift on the royal dome, descending right,
> The bolted valves are pervious to her flight.
> Close to her head the pleasing vision stands,
> And thus performs Minerva's high commands."

The message delivered the phantom departs.

> " The queen awakes, deliver'd of her woes;
> With florid joy her heart dilating glows:
> The vision, manifest of future fate,
> Makes her with hope her son's arrival wait."*

Likewise when Achilles, after the funeral feast of Patroclus, has retired to the shore, and there fallen asleep, he has a dream: the phantom, or shade, of Patroclus, comes to demand the rites of burial:

> " Hush'd by the murmurs of the rolling deep,
> At length he sinks in the soft arms of sleep.
> When lo! the shade before his closing eyes
> Of sad Patroclus rose, or seem'd to rise:
> In the same robe he living wore, he came,
> In stature, voice, and pleasing look, the same."†

The shade pronounced his message, and Achilles making answer begs one last embrace.

> " He said, and with his longing arms essay'd
> In vain to grasp the visionary shade;
> Like a thin smoke he sees the spirit fly,
> And hears a feeble, lamentable cry.

* The Odyssey
† The Iliad.

Confus'd he wakes . . . and exclaims,
' 'Tis true, 'tis certain; man, though dead, retains
Part of himself; th' immortal mind remains:
The form subsists, without the body's aid,
Aërial semblance, and an empty shade!
This night, my friend, so late in battle lost,
Stood at my side, a pensive, plaintive ghost;
E'en now familiar, as in life, he came,
Alas how different! yet how like the same!"

A beautiful example is Perseus' dream, in the pleasant wood at Samos. "A strange dream came to him. . . . There came a lady to him through the wood, taller than he or any mortal man; but beautiful exceedingly, with great gray eyes, clear and piercing. . . . On her head was a helmet, and in her hand a spear. And over her shoulder hung a goat-skin, which bore up a mighty shield of brass, polished like a mirror. . . . Perseus saw that her eyelids never moved, nor her eyeballs, but looked straight through and through him, and into his very heart. . . .

" ' Perseus, you must do an errand for me! '

" ' Who are you lady? And how do you know my name? '

" ' I am Pallas Athene; and I know the thoughts of all men's hearts, and discern their manhood or their baseness. . . . Return to your home, and do the work which waits there for you. You must play the man in that before I can think you worthy to go in search of the Gorgon.'

" Then Perseus would have spoken, but the

strange lady vanished, and he awoke; and behold, it was a dream."*

Jove even sent deceitful visions when they scrved his purpose (the Homeric conception of true dreams coming through the gate of horn, and false through the gate of ivory is based merely on a pun in the Greek). At Thetis' behest, he sends a vision to Agamemnon, prompting him to judge the moment ripe for attacking the Trojans, when in point of fact it was most unpropitious. It is intended to make Agamemnon, in defeat, at last appreciate the true worth of his friend Achilles, Thetis' son, who is sitting apart, neglected and sulky.

> " Now pleasing sleep has seiz'd each mortal eye,
> Stretch't in the tents the Grecian leaders lie.
> Th' immortal slumber'd on their throne above;
> All but the ever-wakeful eyes of Jove.
> To honour Thetis' son he bends his care,
> And plunge the Greeks in all the woes of war:
> Then bids an empty phantom rise to sight:
> And thus commands the vision of the night:
> 'Fly hence, deluding dream! and, light as air,
> To Agamemnon's ample tent repair.
> Bid him in arms draw forth th' embattled train,
> Lead all the Grecians to the dusty plain.
> Declare, e'en now 'tis given him to destroy
> The lofty towers of wide-extended Troy.'
> Swift as the word the vain illusion fled,
> Descends, and hovers o'er Atrides' head;
> Cloth'd in the figure of the Pylian sage,
> Renown'd for wisdom, and rever'd for age;
> Around his temples spreads his golden wing,
> And thus the flatt'ring dream deceives the king."

* Kingsley's " Heroes."

Then the shade " vanish'd from his sight, Resolves
to air, and mixes with the night." Meanwhile
Agamemnon, believing the story true, plans an
attack, and despatches heralds

> " with commands
> To range the camp and summon all the bands."*

But Plato protested against representing the
gods as mere low tricksters. " God is," he wrote,
" a Being of perfect simplicity and truth, . . .
and neither changes in himself nor imposes upon
others, either by apparitions, or by words, or by
sending signs, whether in dreams or in waking
moments. . . . Then while we commend much
in Homer we shall refuse to commend the story
of the dreams sent by Zeus to Agamemnon."†

All these dreams are direct, like Jacob's; but
the symbolic, like Joseph's, also occur, as in the
dream of Hecuba.

> " Queen Hecuba dream'd — an ominous dream of fate—
> That she did bear no human child of flesh,
> But a fierce blazing torch. Priam, alarm'd,
> Ponders with anxious fear the fatal dream;
> And sought the gods with smoking sacrifice. . . .
> Then the diviners' aid he did entreat,
> With many a prayer to the prophetic god,
> If haply he might learn the dream's intent.
> Thus spoke Apollo with all-knowing mind:
> 'The queen shall have a son, who, if he grow
> To man's estate, shall set all Troy in flames —
> The ruin of his city and his land.' "‡

* Iliad.
† " Republic," Book II.
‡ Quoted in Cicero, " De Divinatione."

By the Greek populace the diviner was consulted as we consult a doctor — he was a practical business man, prepared to explain dreams for a fee. His aid was called in as a matter of course and also like a doctor he might disagree with the diagnosis of a fellow practitioner. The night before King Philip married Olympias, the latter dreamed that a thunderbolt fell upon her, " which kindled a great fire, and that the flame extended itself far and wide before it disappeared. And some time after the marriage Philip dreamed that he sealed up the queen's womb with a seal, the impression of which he thought was a lion. Most of the interpreters believed the dream announced some reason to doubt the honour of Olympias, and that Philip ought to look more closely to her conduct. But Aristander of Telmesus, said it only denoted that the queen was pregnant,* for a seal is never put upon anything that is empty; and that the child would prove a boy, of a bold and lionlike courage."*

But far from sharing the superstition of the populace, the great Greek philosophers held various opinions on dreams, substantially agreeing, however, that some were the result of mere animal activities, while others — visions so called — were either divine in origin, or attempts of the soul to know truth.

* Plutarch, " Life of Alexander."

" During the slumbers of that other part of the soul, which is rational and tamed and master of the former, the wild animal part, sated with meat or drink, becomes rampant, and pushing sleep away, endeavors to set out after the gratification of its own proper character. You know that in such moments there is nothing that it dares not do, released and delivered as it is from any sense of shame and reflection. It does not hesitate to commit the foulest murder, or to indulge itself in the most defiling meats. In one word, there is no limit either to its folly or its audacity.

" ' Your description is perfectly true.'

" ' But I imagine, whenever a man's personal habit is healthful and temperate, and when before betaking himself to rest, he has stimulated the rational part of him, and feasted it on beautiful discussions and high inquiries, by means of close and inward reflection; while, on the other hand he has neither stinted nor gorged the appetitive part in order that it may sleep instead of troubling with its joys or its griefs that highest part, which may thus be permitted to pursue its studies in purity and independence, and to strain forward till it perceives something till then unknown, either past, present, or future; and when in like manner, he has calmed the spirited element by avoiding every burst of passion, which would send him to sleep with his spirit stirred, —when, I say, he proceeds to rest, with two elements out of the three quieted, and the third, wherein wisdom resides, aroused, you are aware that, at such moments, he is best able to apprehend truth, and that the visions, which present themselves in his dreams, are then anything but unlawful.'

" ' I perfectly coincide in your opinion.' " *

It has been suggested by scholars that these are rather Socrates' views than Plato's, though the latter records them in " The Republic " and that Plato's real views are those of his "Timæus," in which he disparages dreams as messages only to our lower and irrational nature. As for Aristotle, who entered carefully into the question of sleep, there is no question with him of sanctimonious respect. Dreams, he argues, may sometimes, as all are ready to admit, come true in the sequel, but this is not because they come from God, but either through mere coincidence, or through the extreme sensitiveness of the mind in sleep, by which minute details, unnoticed by day, point to a probable future result, or through the dreamer dwelling on his dream so seriously that he himself brings about the result.   Furthermore, such dreams could not come from God, because He is a rational being, and would certainly grant them only to the wisest and best of men, whereas

* Plato, " Republic," Book IX (Davies and Vaughan's translation).

in point of fact all manner of men claim to have them — and would show some intelligent design, whereas in fact these dreams are sporadic and casual. Essentially Aristotle, like Cicero later, takes the common-sense point of view of a subject only too likely to be exploited by humbug.

The Orphic religion and its descendant, the Pythagorean philosophy, supposing the body " the grave of the soul," conceived sleep as a time of soul-awakening, when converse could be held with heaven. This view found expression in the poets, Pindar and Æschylus, and was general among the Sicilians.

The Greek medical writers also differed greatly on the nature of dreams, some attributing them to excess of supper, others to Jupiter's shades. Hippocrates, for instance, said that during bodily sleep, the soul, being freed from the dominion of the senses, intensified its activity. " When the stars appear (in a dream) to wander this way and that with no necessity, the dream indicates disturbance of the soul due to worry;" and the cure he recommends is laughter and light thoughts. But other dreams, of a nobler sort, are heaven-sent, and can only be explained by a diviner.

But the Greek populace, as we have said, were not so hair-splitting in their distinctions. Sophocles " a learned man, and as a poet quite divine, when a golden goblet of great weight had been stolen from the temple of Hercules, saw in a dream the god himself appearing to him, and declaring who was the robber. Sophocles paid no attention to the vision, though it was repeated more than once. When it had presented itself to him several times, he went up to the court of Areopagus, and laid the matter before them. On this, the judge issued an order for the arrest of the offender nominated by Sophocles. On the application of the torture the criminal confessed his guilt, and restored the goblet from which events this temple of Hercules was afterwards called the temple of Hercules the Indicator."

However, as among the Jews, most dreams were symbolic, and not direct. Prometheus, who taught men the use of fire, claimed also, as he suffered on the mountain crag, " Many modes too of the divining art did I classify, and was the first that discriminated amongst dreams those which are destined to be a true vision." Professional interpreters followed their calling at Athens, and vied with one another in ingenuity of explanation; there were scholarly treatises in existence, and practical manuals (like modern dream books), but they were about as serviceable as " How to Play Golf," or " Swimming Taught in One Lesson."

The dreamer went to an interpreter and told

* Cicero, "De Divinatione," C. D. Yonge's translation.

him his dream. " Was it seen, or heard, — *i. e.*
was it a vision, or an oracle? " the interpreter
would probably ask. " Did it openly foretell the
future, or was it shrouded in symbols? " If it
were a symbolic dream, there would be further
questioning.

" Was it addressed to yourself, your family,
your friends, your country, or the world in general?
What were the circumstances in your experience
that were like those in the dream? "

If the interpretation was still not forthcoming,
the interpreter would scan his lists of previous
examples and meanings of common symbols.
" What are your habits? What is your trade?
Have you any worries? How old are you? Are
you a Greek? " From these he would hope to
gather whether the symbols should be interpreted
favorably or unfavorably, direct or opposite.
Thus, to dream of beheading was generally a bad
omen; but for a prisoner under trial on a capital
charge it was favorable, seeing that no man could
be beheaded twice. To dream of having the nose
cut off meant loss of honor or of life; but a per-
fumer by trade could escape both by shutting up
his shop. To dream of a rainbow was favorable
for a man in trouble, but unfavorable for a contented man.

Interpretations could be obtained also from
the great oracles, like the oracle at Dodona: this

was part of the national religious system, and therefore orthodox. The Greeks in fine, except for occasional advanced thinkers, held dreams in high esteem as regular channels of communication with their divinities.

Much the same views appear to have held sway in Rome; with perhaps more skepticism. Pliny, following Plato, attributed dreams after heavy meals to the ordinary operations of the mind, but other dreams to divine interposition; Cicero attributed all dreams to natural causes, uninfluenced by the divine. The populace went, as in Athens, to professional diviners.

In the writings of the Christian fathers, we find warning after warning against placing our trust in false dreams and false prophets; yet even they allowed many dreams to be divine.

Tertullian (160-240 A.D.) held the view that like the body the soul took nourishment during sleep, but of a different kind, consisting of dreams. Dreams were natural, not a violation of nature like the hallucinations of insanity; in them revelations might be made, of medical treatment, hidden treasure, stolen goods, or future honors; demons might cause impure, frivolous, or turbulent dreams; and visions containing sacred prophecy, might proceed from holy angels and the Father Himself.*

* " De Anima."

Porphyry (232 A.D.) a Platonic philosopher of the Alexandrian school ascribed dreams to the agency of a good demon, who used them to give us warning against the practices of an evil demon.

Lactantius (325 A.D.) affirmed his belief in the divine origin of certain dreams, and based it on the evidence of sacred and profane history; he agreed with Vergil, that dreams are neither always true nor always untrue. * Synesius of Cyrene (370–413 A.D.), another Alexandrian, extolled divination by dreams in a treatise that he wrote one night in a dream vigil; he said it was the simplest and surest method of prophesying the future. In a word, the Fathers did not deny the truth of visions, but insisted on care being taken that mere dreams should not be mistaken for them.

The Middle Ages was the period *par excellence* of bad dreams, demons excelling angels in activity; and the gargoyles of Notre Dame — or of English churches, such as the parish church at Winchcombe — perpetuate their grotesque appearance.

The Schoolmen inquired into the nature of dreams, in answer to the question of St. Thomas Aquinas (1226–1274), " Is divination through dreams unlawful? " His own answer was, " It depends on the source of the particular dream." Some dreams are animal, the product of such

* " De Opificio Dei."

factors as memories, health and posture; these cannot instruct us in the knowledge of the spiritual world. Others are incorporeal, and must be ascribed to the agency of angels, devils, or God Himself; these must be solemnly attended to. The dreamer's duty is to decide the class to which his dream belongs, and only from dreams of the second class to divine the future.

That this view did not utterly die out with the Middle Ages we have abundant evidence; thus it was fully endorsed as late as the seventeenth century by a famous English physician and scholar, who says, " That there should be divine dreams seems unreasonably doubted by Aristotle. That there are demoniacal dreams we have little reason to doubt. Why may there not be angelical? If there be guardian spirits, they may not be inactively about us in sleep; but may sometimes order our dreams; and many strange hints, instigations, or discourses, which are so amazing unto us, may arise from such foundations."*

However, in the Middle Ages, this view was widely held; and, with fear of the supernatural very prevalent, nightmares were extraordinarily common. Innumerable people dreamed of demonic embraces; they woke up exhausted after a seeming struggle, and seemed to see the tormentor hastening away, tail, horns and all. Visions were no

* Sir Thomas Browne.

uncommon experience. Wizards and witches were
feared and put to a shameful death. Superstition
knew no bounds.

In Teutonic countries, dreams of communication
with gods were unknown till the arrival of Christianity, and the general type was an omen of
impending evil. However, guardian spirits might
appear, and deceased members of the dreamer's
family, to give warning of some danger, like a
landslip or fire, threatening the sleeper's fortunes.
In keeping with the gloomy nature of most of
the Teutonic dreams of which we have record,
the dreamer seldom profited by his warning, but
fell a prey to misfortune in spite of it. After the
coming of Christianity, visions do occur, but they
cannot be said to be a native product. Nightmares
were not considered a similar phenomenon to
dreams, but either the actual presence of a supernatural being, or else the practices of witchcraft.

Throughout Western civilization, in modern
times, the belief in dreams as channels of intercourse with supernatural powers has been widely
held, though divorced from medicine, philosophy
and religion; and today one is continually meeting
people that are ready to vouch for the truth of
dreams of the sort; indeed, so dear to us all is
the extraordinary that it will be a long time before
the belief dies out. Perhaps *the* typical example
of modern supernatural dreams is the Swaffham

tinker's, which is like thousands current in conversation if not in books.

Once a certain tinker, of Swaffham in Norfolk, dreamed that he was told to go on a journey to London, and stand at a certain point on London Bridge, where he would be met by some one that would tell him news of great importance to his future. The tinker's wife teased him about the dream, but when it was repeated the next night, and the night following, he was so powerfully moved that, in spite of his wife's complaints and his neighbors' ridicule, he did actually set off for London.

In three days time he finished the ninety-mile tramp; and next morning he took up his station on the bridge, which (for he had never seen it before) was in appearance exactly as he had dreamed it to be. He waited all day long, but nobody accosted him; the second day it was the same; and the third day, too.

Late at night with his mind made up to go home next day, he began to quit his stand on the bridge, when a stranger accosted him and inquired what he had been standing about for so long. Without giving names and details, the tinker told the stranger why he had come there, while the latter burst out laughing at him for a fool, and bade him go back home and be wiser for the future. " I, myself," said he, " were I disposed to trust such things, might now go a hundred miles into the country on just such an errand as yours; for three nights this week have I dreamed that if I went to a town called Swaffham, in Norfolk, and there dug under an apple-tree in a certain garden on the north side of the town, I should find a chest of money; but I have something else to do than to run after such idle fancies! No, no, my friend; go back home and work hard at your calling, and you will find there the riches that you have come here to seek."

The tinker, concluding this to be the message he had come for, thanked the stranger for his advice; and next morning he set out for home. At Swaffham he kept his own counsel, got up early in the morning, and began digging at the spot the stranger had described. A few feet down, his spade (of course) struck against something hard, which proved to be an iron chest, which he soon hauled up and bore home. The chest contained a pile of money, and an inscription; the latter he could not read, but some boys from the local Grammar School told him it read,

> " Where this stood
> Is another twice as good."

He went back to the apple-tree and dug again, and found a second chest, twice as big, and bursting with gold and silver.

The tinker was now well off, and made a thank

offering to God in the form of a new chancel in
the parish church. Nowadays a monument in
the church, consisting of a marble effigy of the
tinker and his dog, with a tinker's outfit, is still
pointed out as his.*

The favorite field of these dreams is, however,
that of crime, the most popular story being the
Red Barn Mystery or the Murder of Maria
Marten.

Maria Marten, of Polstead in Suffolk, ran away
(in 1827) with William Corder, a farmer, who
betrayed her, murdered her, and buried her under
the floor of a barn. Corder kept out of the way,
and wrote to the Martens saying his wife was
keeping well; and so for nearly a year nobody
suspected the crime.

One night Maria's mother dreamed she saw
the murder, and the burial of her daughter under
the barn floor. On April 19, 1828, Mr. Marten,
on account of what his wife had dreamed, broke
up the barn floor, and found the body in a sack,
very much decayed, but able to be identified by
the teeth of which two, in a certain position,
had been drawn. Corder, who was now married
and living in Essex, was arrested, and tried; he
confessed in prison, and was executed in August,
1828.

There is no end to the similar cases on record,

* See Blomfield's " History of Norfolk," p. 215 *et seq.*

which are quite a sufficient justification for the
common use of the dream in literature. Whether
the real cause is premonition or coincidence is
not of the least importance; the mystery and
miraculousness of the stories lend them an interest
which none of us would care to miss; and it is
only a hard, unimaginative mind that, having a
theory of the real truth, would altogether discard
the tales as idle inventions.

Of course, we do not find many records of the
innumerable prophetic dreams that do *not* come
true. " Men dream", says MacNish, " every now
and then, that they will die on a certain day,
yet how seldom do we see those predictions
fulfilled by the result! " Morbid people commonly
think such things; while their practical friends
either laugh them out of it, or put the clock back
at the fatal moment, and then inform them that
the moment is over. Certain diseases cause apprehensive and unpleasant dreams that are naturally
interpreted by credulous busybodies to mean an
early death; and as the forecast is generally
true, the superstitious once more claim a victory.

The truth is that when the mind (as Bacon wrote
in the " Novum Organum ") " is once pleased
with certain things, it draws all others to consent,
and go along with them; and though the power
and number of instances that make for the contrary are greater, yet it either attends not to them,

or despises them, or else removes them by a distinction, with a strong and pernicious prejudice to maintain the authority of the first choice inviolated. And hence in most cases of superstition, as of Astrology, Dreams, Omens, Judgments, etc., those who find pleasure in such kinds of vanities, always observe where the event answers, but slight and pass by the instances where it fails, which are much the more numerous."

CHAPTER IV

DREAM-PROCURING

*"The priest on skins of offering takes his ease
And nightly visions in his slumbers sees." — Dryden.*

FEED a dog once or twice at table, as a special
favor, and soon he will come of his own accord,
and insist on it as a right; so, vouchsafe certain
men divine dreams, and soon they will not only
anticipate but solicit them. The practice of performing ritual, and supplicating the gods, in
order to obtain dreams in which cures of diseases
are accorded, was formerly widespread, and called
incubation.

There were reasons for preferring incubated
to freely vouchsafed dreams; incubation brought
the dreamer into contact with the particular deity
concerned with his kind of disease, and obtained
a direct categorical answer to a direct categorical
question. Soliciting healing dreams naturally
grew into a cult, as in Greece, and was very
profitable to the priestly class.

Incubation is of very early origin and existed
in an advanced state in ancient Egypt, where it
was a common practice among all classes. Inscrip-

tions have been discovered and deciphered, conveying vivid impressions of the process, which was elaborate. The patient first entered one of the sanctuaries of a temple where the gods were wont to grant responses, and prayed fervently to the deity beseeching him by his celebrated virtues, to reveal himself. " Turn thy face towards us," he said, " for 'tis thou who dost accomplish miracles and art benevolent in all thy doings "; or, " 'Tis thou who hast created magic, and established the heavens and the earth and the lower world; 'tis thou who canst grant me the means of saving all." Having next adjured the god to " hear the prayer," the suppliant laid votive offerings on the altar, and, having probably fasted, waited for the god to come and answer him in his sleep.

Then, in a dream the god appeared, the inscriptions going on to say, "The god X—— spake to him, saying, ' Art thou not such an one, son (or father, or wife, and so on) of so-and-so? ' " The reply being " Yes," the god then instructed the sleeper in simple words what to do when morning should come; thus he might say that at a certain given spot a sealed box would be found, containing a certain book which was to be copied and replaced, after which there would be a certain given result.

In Greece, incubation was an integral part of the religious code, not universally obligatory, but, in conjunction with festival-keeping, a form of extra-ordinary ritual. The original belief was that earth would give prophetic visions, under certain conditions; later it was believed to be some god or other, especially Æsculapius, that granted, on ground consecrated to him, dreams of prescriptions for ailments. Thus oracles sprang up at favored spots like Delphi, which was sacred to Apollo.

The oracles were situated in places where local conditions favored dreams, lonely caverns, enervating valleys, regions of gaseous escape, and ghastly cliffs and gorges, being especially well suited to the purpose. The deities of the oracles were the heroes and lesser gods of Greek mythology; and answers on public calamities and national scourges could be obtained, as well as prescriptions for diseases. At certain of the Greek oracles, as in the Babylonian and Chaldean, the responses were delivered by dreams to priestesses who lived alone in temples as the concubines of the gods; at others, as in the Egyptian, the suppliants were themselves granted the dreams, which might, however, require interpreting by the attendant priests.

One of the well-thronged Greek oracles was that of Oropus, dedicated to Amphiaraus, a deified magician. The patient came to the Amphiaræum, or temple, and fasted a whole day for purification; then he sacrificed a ram to the hero, and lay down on the outstretched skin to sleep. On awakening afterwards, he told his dream to the officiating priest, who interpreted it for him.

It was somewhat similar at Lebadea, where there was an oracle of Trophonius, but the rites were stricter. After purification, the suppliant bathed and anointed himself, and, with a honeyed cake held in his hand, descended into a cave, where he lay and fell asleep. On awakening afterwards, feeling depressed (through the gases in the air), he got up and took a seat dedicated to Mnesmosyne, and retailed his dream. Next he was led by the priests to the Chapel of Good Fortune, where he became brighter in spirits, and was informed what the interpretation was.

The most famous of the oracles was at Epidaurus, sacred to Æsculapius, the father of medicine. There the patient slept in a special temple, the " abaton," and supplicated a cure. The responses were twofold, one a dream, the other a cure, and he woke up to find himself whole; the dream consisting in the appearance of the god or a sacred animal (a snake for instance), which touched the diseased place in the body, and so healed it up. In later days, it was the priests that dreamed, and they instructed the patient how to obtain a cure.

The machinery of dream oracles is obvious.

Potent gases, or other contributory influences, stimulated vivid dreams, the frightful aspect of wild and secluded places inspired awe, and pre-occupation with religious ideas lent a divine color to the experience; fasting and narcotic potions increased the ecstasy; and then faith, strengthened by the prestige of the oracle, and the manipulation of the diseased place by the priests, brought about the cures.

There is an inscription extant, recording the cure of blindness in a woman at Epidaurus. In her dream she saw the divine Æsculapius, who addressed her in words, and admonished her for her want of faith; she vowed to atone for her defection by dedicating a silver pig (his sacred animal) to his name, and when he dropped a healing lotion on her eyes, her sight was instantly restored. Also, a woman afflicted with worms dreamed that Æsculapius approached, performed an operation on her, and having extracted the worms, stitched up the wound he had made. A man with moles on his forehead saw Æsculapius come up and tie a bandage round his head; the bandage was afterwards taken off, leaving the forehead smooth, and itself retaining the moles. These cures would appear to be brought about by a slight surgical operation, while the patient dosed with a narcotic, was sleeping heavily.

Such a vogue did oracles obtain that in some

instances the Early Christian Church maintained them, when the old religion passed away, with saints of the Church in place of the old pagan deities. In Byzantium, two churches, erected on spots consecrated to the Argonauts, were dedicated by the Emperor Constantine to the Archangel Michael; and it was traditionally said that the oracle had prophesied a new consecration, to an incorruptible god whose word should become flesh in a virgin (Mary, it was assumed, though Rhea was more probable). In time these churches became centers of healing miracles and angelic visions, something like the modern Lourdes, and formed a species of Christian oracle, — the dreams being attributed to the Archangel Michael instead of to the pagan Apollo and Serapis. One of the cases of which we have record was of a patient who, " being as if half-dead, ordered a servant to bear him to the church, in the hope of a cure taking place there, or of ending his agony in death. After reaching the place, God appeared to him in the night, and bade him drink a draught compounded of honey, pepper and wine. He did so, and was thereupon restored to health."*

Similarly a church at Aegæ in Cilicia, where an oracle of Æsculapius had been, and where two martyrs had suffered death under Diocletian, was dedicated to the saints of Byzantium, and

* La Magie et L'Astrologie," by L.-E. Alfred Maury, Paris, 1879.

suffered a re-transformation into an oracle. It was said that the saints of Byzantium appeared one night in a dream to the Emperor Justinian, as he lay seriously ill in bed; and he awoke whole. As the report of the miracle spread, the shrine became the goal of throngs of pilgrims, who came to invoke the saints for cures: and cures there were, innumerable, with the result that the oracle was restored to its former popularity and function, but in disguised form — it had changed hands, that was all.

The Teutonic peoples do not appear, before the advent of Christianity, to have practised incubation or to have conceived of dreams as messages from the gods. There is something akin, however, to a procured dream in the Vatnsdaela Saga, in the story of the Norwegian chief Ingimund. Ingimund proposed to settle in Iceland, and adopted an original method of procuring first hand information about the lay of the country; for he had three Finns kept under close guard in a hut, and ordered to go to sleep there, while their souls set out for Iceland, and chose out a suitable district to colonize. To give adequate time for the long journey, three nights were granted for the sleep. The prisoners obeyed the order; and after three nights they awoke, and, reporting their souls' return, described what they had seen in Iceland. And all seems to have been well and true.

Such customs as have been described above, while not now existing in the same form, have rather changed their activities than died out altogether. In quite recent times the Ankaras and Big Belly Indians, before going on the warpath, used to fast and have a vision of the success or failure of the expedition, wise men of the tribes reading the interpretation. And at the present day, St. Agnes' and Midsummer Eve customs are oracular, like all the beliefs in the procuring of dreams of future wife or husband; they are helps to life, they stimulate healthy curiosity and hope, and form part of the play of natural man.

Midsummer Eve is a favorite occasion for these practices. In parts of Wales, there is a belief that if a sprig of mistletoe picked on that eve is laid under the pillow, dreams of the future will attend the sleep. It was believed within living memory, at Pulverbatch (in Shropshire), that the oak tree blossoming on Midsummer Eve, but the blooms withering before morning, if a maid would like to know who her future husband was to be, she should go at night and spread a cloth beneath the oak: she would find a little dust, the relics of the blossoms, on the cloth next morning, and if she laid them under her pillow, she would dream of her future husband.

Hallowe'en is oracular as well, in some districts. In County Leitrim, if a girl found a branch of briar twisted backwards and growing into the ground, to form a loop with the trunk, and she crept three times, in the devil's name, through the loop, snapped off the bough and took it home to put under her pillow, unknown to any one else she would dream that night of her future husband. Youths procured dreams of love and marriage in a different way; they silently gathered ten leaves of ivy, threw one away, and put the remaining nine under their pillow. This hocus-pocus is as oracular, and almost as ritualistic, as the Greek.

Hallowe'en has a following in South Uist and Eriskay also, two of the Outer Hebrides. They eat a cake made of meal and salt, and then, silent and thirsty go off to sleep and dream of the future; or else they bolt down a whole salted herring in three bites, keep silent, drink nothing and go off to sleep, when dreams of the future are procured.

The St. Agnes' Eve custom is immortalized in Keats' poem. Madeline being instructed in the lore of the oracle, unforeseen circumstances bring about a true answer.

> " They told her how, upon St. Agnes' Eve,
>   Young virgins might have visions of delight,
>   And soft adorings from their loves receive
>   Upon the honey'd middle of the night,
>   If ceremonies due they did aright;
>   As, supperless to bed they must retire,
>   And couch supine their beauties, lily white;
>   Nor look behind, nor sideways, but require
>   Of Heaven with upward eyes for all that they desire.

Full of this whim was thoughtful Madeline . . .
She sigh'd for Agnes' dreams, the sweetest of the year."

Such are only a few of the thousand oracles of modern times, of which there are vestiges still in every country; and two more will show other typical methods of obtaining responses. " 'Tis a custom among country-girls to put the Bible under their pillows at night, with sixpence clapt in the book of Ruth, in order to dream of the man destined to be their husbands."* " Writing their name on a paper at twelve o'clock, burning the same, then carefully gathering up the ashes, and laying them close wrapp'd in a paper upon a looking-glass, marked with a cross, under their pillows, this should make them dream of their love."

That oracles in one shape or another should have persisted through thousands of years of man's history, up to this present day, is enough proof that they answer some universal desire of mankind, — the desire to peer into the future, and the desire to have a cure for diseases or troubles from sources not limited like human ones. It is an excusable weakness of man, to jump at even the remotest chance of finding out the unknown and predestined; and oracles, in one form or another, will exist probably as long as the human race itself.

* " Poems by Nobody," London, 1770.

CHAPTER V

DREAMS AS OMENS

Uncle — " So you believe in dreams coming true, do you, Betty? "
Betty — " Of course. Why last night I dreamt I'd been paddling —
and I had." — "Punch," Summer Number, 1920.

" Leuconoé dear, seek not I pray to know
    What Heaven hath hid;
The span to me accorded, or to thee,
    Is lore forbid!
Tempt not Chaldean horoscopes! More wise
    What comes, to bear;

Nor fret, whether some winters more from Jove
    Fall to our share,
Or this, which lashes now the Tuscan shore
    Our last decreed —
Seize now and here the hour that is, nor trust
    Some later day! " — *Horace.*

THE oracle degenerates into the love dream of
St. Agnes' Eve; the interpretation of sacred visions
into the quackery of popular dream books. When
dreams were universally venerated, a distinction
was drawn between divine visions and normal
dreams; but in the decadence of the faith a meaning is ascribed to *all* dreams, and future events are
forecasted with no thought of consulting the will
of the gods.

The interpretation of dreams early became
methodized and mechanical, the Arabs and·

Persians forming special codes; and Artemidorus early formulating rules in his dream classic, the "Oneirocritica." However often in practice the code proves wanting, there are always sufficient coincidences in life to insure that a true forecast will be made sometimes; and then credulity is satisfied, and tides over its disappointment till the next true forecast happens. There is more joy in the heart of the credulous over one interpretation that comes true than disappointment over ninety-and-nine interpretations that do *not* come true. " I am extremely surprised," wrote Cicero, " that though people have wit enough to give no credit to a notorious liar, even when he speaks the truth, they still, if one single dream has turned out true, do not so much distrust one single case because of the numbers of instances in which they have been found false, as think multitudes of dreams established because of the ascertained truth of this one."

Dream books also owe their popularity to another characteristic of dreams, namely, that they tend to be of some things more than others, and so a list of common symbols can be drawn up. It is an easy step then to draw up a key book of interpretations.

Most people dream at some time or other of falling off a bridge, or over a cliff, having a tooth pulled out, swimming and flying, wandering about

half-clothed, and missing an appointment; and one can easily draw up " model answers " to these, as there is no necessity for the " answers " to be true. However, little allowance can be made in such a scheme for the dreamer's ideas and affairs, as there had been in the diagnosis of skilled interpreters; and the same answer is made to the same dream for every one. If six people take a flight in an aeroplane, it is not implied that they all go for the same purpose; one may want to reach a certain place, another to learn to fly, a third to win a wager, a fourth to feel the thrill, a fifth to satisfy curiosity, and a sixth to carry a message. Each flyer would have a different association with the flight, and so with dreams of flying; but a dream book takes no account of this. However, it is more elastic than the old rule of thumb, " Ne'er fear it, dreams go by the contraries;"* which looks like the cynical reflection of the wiseacres that notice the exceptions, and is the dream faith held widely " by the common people of Europe." †
Filth betokens money to come; friends, making enemies; and the best dream to have is of wallowing up to the neck in the mire: and obviously a dream book could be drawn up on this principle alone.

Dream books derive their interpretations from

* Wycherley's "Gentleman Dancing Master," Act IV, Scene 1.
† "Memories of Extraordinary Popular Delusions and the Madness of Crowds," by Charles Mackay, 1892.

the associations of the thing dreamed about; and this is an ancient practice. " Many dreams," wrote Sir Thomas Browne (in the seventeenth century), " are made out by sagacious exposition, and from the signature of their subjects; carrying their interpretation in their fundamental sense and mystery of similitude, whereby, he that understands upon what natural fundamental every notional dependeth, may, by symbolical adaptation, hold a ready way to read the characters of Morpheus. In dreams of such a nature, Artemidorous, Achmet, and Astrampsichus, from Greek, Egyptian, and Arabian oneiro-criticism, may hint some interpretation: who, while we read of a ladder in Jacob's dream, will tell us that ladders and scaling ascents signify preferment; and while we consider the dream of Pharaoh, do teach us that rivers overflowing speak plenty, lean oxen, famine and scarcity; and therefore it was but reasonable in Pharaoh to demand the interpretation from his magicians, who, being Egyptians, should have been well versed in symbols and the hieroglyphical notions of things. The greatest tyrant in such divination was Nabuchodonosor, while, besides the interpretation, he demanded the dream itself; which being probably determined by divine immission, might escape the common road of phantasms, that might have been traced by Satan."

Dream books are very common today, and go by all sorts of mystic names, like Raphael and Napoleon's Book of Fate. In the introduction to Raphael's Dream Book, it is stated that dreams, as the Bible gives warrant, foretell the future. There are two methods of procedure: one for dreams that are intricate or forgotten, and the other, by the chief images seen, for clear and simple dreams.

The first method is an ingenious game of hazard. You write down ten rows of noughts, one row below another, with a space between the fifth and sixth. The number of noughts in any line is left to your caprice.

Let these be the ten rows:

000000000000	12 ciphers, or even	00	
000000000	9 ciphers, or odd	0	
000000000000000	15 ciphers, or odd	0	} Sign One
000000	6 ciphers, or even	00	
0000000000	10 ciphers, or even	00	
00000000000000	14 ciphers, or even	00	
00000000000	11 ciphers, or odd	0	
0000000000000	13 ciphers, or odd	0	} Sign Two
00000000000000	14 ciphers, or even	00	
000000000000	12 ciphers, or even	00	

You add up the noughts in the first line, as shown above, write down the total, together with a statement whether it is odd or even: even numbers are symbolized by two ciphers, odd numbers by one. You treat the whole ten lines in the same way, and then call the first five symbols, Sign One, and the second five, Sign Two. Sign One and Sign Two are now placed side by side, and added together line by one to form the index, as below.

Sign One	Sign Two		Index
0 0	0 0	=4 cyphers, or even	0 0
0	0	=2 cyphers, or even	0 0
0	0	=2 cyphers, or even	0 0
0 0	0 0	=4 cyphers, or even	0 0
0 0	0 0	=4 cyphers, or even	0 0

Now that the index is known, you turn to the part of the dream book containing indexes, and glance over them until you find the right one. The index book is called the Hieroglyphical Emblem of Aries. You now turn to the " interpretations " page of " Aries," and scan the collection of signs till you find Sign One and Sign Two; and then you read, " An uncommon omen; cares and toils are denoted. A harassing time after this dream. Be very careful."

This is the essence of fatuous mystification, but there is a certain excitement in puzzling it out. The second method, for remembered dreams, has no mystery in it, but more sense; it consists in turning up an alphabetical list of symbols till you find the one that was principal in your dreams, and then reading the interpretation. A similar list is given in " Napoleon's Book of Fate, Captured at the Battle of Leipsic, with Interpretations of Dreams." The associations used are of several kinds, but the direct association is common.

" *Bomb*. If a fair maiden should dream of seeing a bombshell, she must look out for a brave artilleryman coming to ask her to be his bride. If she dreams she sees one of these articles explode, she will have great peace and comfort in her married life, a fond and faithful husband, and a happy family of handsome and dutiful sons and blooming daughters."

" If you dream that you are walking, and your way is frequently intercepted by hedges, it implies that you will meet with great opposition in business and love."

" *Flying*. For any one to dream of flying implies that they are aspiring to something they will never be able to attain, and unless speedily abandoned, will end in their discomfiture and ruin."

" *Harp*. For a young woman to dream that she plays on a harp means that in her married life she will have much joy and harmony; in her union she will have a very good, true and honourable pianomaker for a husband." So low has dream interpretation fallen since Joseph's time!

Contrary associations (as in the second part of the above) are also common; so under " *Fortune*," is given, " To dream of having a fortune left you is a very bad sign, being a sure forerunner of pecuniary loss and embarrassment. . . . To persons with large families the dream indicates that their children will form unfortunate engagements, and other calamities which our limits will not permit us to specify." "Which our limits will not permit us to specify"!

"*Gorilla.* For a young woman to dream that she is in love with, and embraced by a gorilla, means that she will have one of the handsomest and wisest men in the neighborhood for a suitor, and will be envied by all the marriageable ladies in the district."

Yet other symbols are interpreted by the wishes and hopes they represent. "*Palace.* To dream that you are in a palace is a good omen, showing a speedy advancement in your circumstances, and position in society, and also that you will marry very well."

"For a young woman to dream . . . "; this popular commencement reveals the public really intrigued by this romantic pastime.

Of the two most common dreams, the dream book offers the following interpretations, both most unfavorable.

"*Falling.* Nothing can be more unfavorable than to dream of falling from any place, in all cases it implies a loss of situation and property. Young persons need never expect to be united to the object of their affections after such a dream."

" *Naked*. To dream that you are in a state of nudity is a dream of bad omen, foretelling to a certainty, poverty, disgrace, and misfortune. . . . To persons in love it shows that they will never marry the present object of their affections, but the person they will get will be cross-tempered, unkind and extravagant, and will, in a great measure, be the means of bringing you to poverty."

The book having been opened at random and the first twenty answers taken, the following was found to be the percentage of different kinds — a pretty safe test of what the commonest answers are:

Of children, five per cent,
Of disappointment, ten per cent,
Of misfortunes, ten per cent,
Of riches, ten per cent,
Of married life, fifteen per cent,
Of good fortune, twenty-five per cent,
Of lovers, seventy-five per cent,
Of death, five per cent,
Of enemies, ten per cent,
Of obstacles, ten per cent.

So the answers are arranged to make the chances high for good fortune and a love affair, things which are well suited to please any reader; and one need not fear the dreadful effects that Addison waxed so furious about in his " Essay on Popular Superstitions."

Addison attributed the curiosity which is the motive of people who try to peer into the future to " that fear and ignorance which are natural to the soul of man. The horror with which we entertain the thoughts of death (or indeed of any future evil), and the uncertainty of its approach, fill a melancholy mind with innumerable apprehensions and suspicions, and consequently dispose it to the observation of such groundless prodigies and predictions. For as it is the chief concern of wise men to retrench the evils of life by the reasonings of philosophy: it is the employment of fools to multiply them by the sentiments of superstition." And he adds, exhibiting his own not very human nature, " For my own part, I should be very much troubled were I endowed with this divining quality, though it should inform me truly of everything that can befall me. I would not anticipate the relish of any happiness, nor feel the weight of any misery, before it actually arrives."

Old dream books, if not so obviously fobbed up to attract serving maids and country girls, were much after the same style as those described above. Milton's " Astrologaster," for example, has the following examples:* "19. That to dreame of the devil is good lucke. 20. That to dreame of gold is good luck, but of silver ill." " The Country-

* Page 45, number 13.

man's Counsellor," published in London in 1633, says that, " To dreame of eagles flying over our heads, to dreame of marriages, dancing and banquetting, foretells some of our kinsfolk are departed; to dreame of silver, if thou hast it given to thyself, sorrow; of gold, good fortune; to lose an axle tooth or an eye, the death of some friend; to dreame of bloody teeth the death of the dreamer "; and so on.

And these readings are modeled on interpretations commonly believed in Europe, and anterior to printed dream books. In various parts of Europe, they believe that to dream of little pigs is fortunate; bullocks, unfortunate; a house on fire means news from a far country; vermin means sickness in the family; serpents, friends will turn out to bitter enemies; and there is no better dream than of wallowing up to your neck in mud.* Clear waters means sorrow; running naked in the streets, troubles and perplexity.

In England, the oak means long life and prosperity; in Switzerland, calamity. Stripping the bark off a tree means loss of character to a maiden, family bereavement to a mother, a rich legacy to a man. Anemones mean love; bilberries, an excursion; broom, a baby; lilies, joy; water-lilies, danger from the sea; lemons, separation; violets; bad luck to the single, good luck to the married,

* Mackay's " Memories of Extraordinary Popular Delusions."

yellow flowers, jealousy; daffodils, the good angel
warns a maiden to beware of her lover; the advice
neglected,

> " Never again shall she put garland on;
> Instead of it she'll wear sad cypress now,
> And bitter elder broken from the bough."

But the meanings are very capricious; an English
girl will be lucky if she dreams of a rose, a Norman
girl will be unlucky.

Such is the decadence of the religious vision —
a mere mechanical omen, beloved by the ignorant
and credulous. Dreams began by being real and
obvious; they became real and not obvious; and
last they became not real and not obvious: first
they were self-explanatory; then they required
explaining; last, they became mechanical omens,
interpreted according to plan.

The evolution of the dream theory up to this
point may be marked in a single race in the history
of the Jewish views of dreams. Originally, no
doubt, the Jews understood dreams literally as
sorties of the soul, with vivid excitements like
those of the day, yet in some mysterious way
unlike. Later, they accounted them supernatural
visitations, or visions, some of them self-explanatory, and others enigmatic without the interpretation of seers. Dream interpreting became a
profession — like medicine; and the Jews of Pales-
tine and Babylon, during the first five centuries

of the Christian era, consulted interpreters about their dreams as we consult doctors about our diseases, bad dreams being treated with a special fast. Dreamers could not perform their own interpretations, but only the feed interpreters and it was worth while to pay a good sum, as the dreams inevitably " came true " according to the interpretation that was given. " A dream not interpreted," declared Hesda, a third-century Babylonian Jew, " is like a letter not read"; the standard fee in his day was one denarius, and there were twenty-four official interpreters in the city of Jerusalem.

In the next stage of its development, the dream was a mere omen. If a superstitious Jew had a bad dream, he fasted next day to appease the ruler of dreams; but the Jews of Minsk, with a characteristic business cunning, had a recipe for avoiding the consequence, *viz.*, to repeat the following charm, " God is master, The dream is a fool; Whatever I dream tonight, I will not fast tomorrow," so that the ruler of dreams would conclude it a waste of time to send them a bad one. It is still believed amongst certain of the Russian Jews, that dreams obtain their fulfilment according to the interpretation first given; from which is derived their proverb, " Don't tell your dream to a fool." The Eastern Jews have a dream book, (of which an edition was published at

Brooklyn so recently as in 1902, translated into Yiddish from Almoli's " Pitron Halomot " — Almoli lived in Constantinople), in which dreams are classified according to subjects, such as animals, plants, the dead, angels, and there is a fixed interpretation — an ox that gores the dreamer means long life, demons mean success in money affairs, a dead man carrying fruit means that he is in heaven — and falling through space means that he is driven out of heaven.

The last stage is the skeptical and rational; wonder and awe yield place to materialistic investigation. Yet Dr. Henri Jung, one of the most advanced dream investigators of the present day writes in a recent book,* " We find to our astonishment that an apparently senseless dream is quite full of sense, and deals with extraordinarily important and serious problems of the soul. Having acquired this knowledge we cannot refrain from giving rather more credit to the old superstitions concerning the meaning of dreams for which our rationalizing tendencies, until lately, had no use."

* " New Paths in Psychology."

CHAPTER VI

Dreams as Thought

"To dream is nothing else but to think sleeping."
— *De Foe*, Hist. Devil. **1726.**

" Those dreams that on the silent night intrude.
    And with false flitting shades our mind delude,
Jove never sends us downward from the skies;
    Nor can they from infernal mansions rise;
But all are mere productions of the brain,
And fools consult interpreters in vain." — *Swift*, "On Dreams."

THERE have always been, and it is probable that there always will be, those who believe in the supernatural origin of dreams; but there have been others, and their number has kept on increasing, who do not. The latter hold all manner of different views on the subject, but they have one thing in common: they consider dreams to be products of the brain, like thought and feeling; they are materialists satisfied that if everything about dreams were known, they would be found to be phenomena with assignable normal causes, operating according to universal laws. This is the " scientific " stage of dream theory. A child willingly believes in Father Christmas, who comes down the chimney and fills his stocking, but a grown-up man does not: he is materialistic enough to say that Father Christmas is just a very ordinary man playing a poetic prank with his children, with an unspoken " Let us pretend " in his heart. We have now to deal, in like manner, with the grown-up view of the dream.

The scientific views of the dream are as many and various as the supernatural. " As to the cause of dreams," wrote Cornelius Agrippa, " both external and internal, they do not all agree in one judgment. . . . For the Platonics reckon them among the specific and concrete notions of the soul. Avicen makes the cause of dreams to be an ultimate intelligence moving the moon in the middle of that light with which the fancies of men are illuminate while they sleep. Aristotle refers the cause thereof to common sense, but placed in the fancy. Averroes places the cause in the imagination. Democritus ascribes it to little images or representatives separated from the things themselves; Albertus to the superior influences that continually flow from the sky through many specific mediums. The physicians impute the cause thereof to vapors and humors; others to the affections and cares predominant in persons when awake. Others joyn the powers of the soul, celestial influences, and images together, all making but one cause."

Nowadays, most people are ready to assume, without giving any thought to the subject, that dreams are a natural product, with nothing miraculous about them. It was not always so: the supernatural theory of " celestial influences " had to be strongly combated, before an opinion contary to it dare be expressed.

One of the most forcible of the attacks on the supernatural theory was delivered nearly two thousand years ago by Cicero, in his book " De Diviniatione." The attack opens advisedly from the supernatural camp, in the person of Quintus, Cicero's brother, who advances a batch of unconvincing arguments in favor of the theory of divine intervention; and then Marcus Tullius opposes them, armed to the teeth with counter-arguments.

In the first place, he argues, in our everyday experience we suffer innumerable hallucinations, like that of a candle-flame's looking double; then why should we suppose that, of all these hallucinations, dreams alone require the intervention of divine power, or alone are the vehicle of divine messages? Madmen dream mad dreams, but we do not say that *they* are true; then why should we arrogate to our own dreams the only truth?

If we would play on any instrument, practice composition, deliver speeches, or acquire scholarship, we apply ourselves laboriously to study; yet we expect, complacently enough, to learn a certain and instant cure for any and all diseases by merely consulting an oracle! Moreover, suppose the gods *did* favor one suppliant with an answer, while another was denied, would that not be unfair and ungodlike? And why should sensible gods send these dreams while we are asleep, and least in a condition, therefore, to profit by them, when they could just as well send them while we are awake or alert?

Certain authorities divide dreams into two categories, the false and the true, the latter of divine origin; then whence come the false? If they also come from the gods, then the gods are inconsistent and unworthy of respect; and if they come from nature, the gods are still inconsistent, confusing direct operations with indirect: therefore all dreams must proceed from nature.

" Which is more probable; that the supreme and immortal gods who excel in every kind of superiority employ themselves in visiting all night long not merely the beds, but the very pallets of men, and as soon as they find any person fairly snoring, entertain his imagination with perplexed dreams of obscure visions, which sends him in great alarm as soon as daylight dawns to consult the seer and interpreter; or whether these dreams are the result of natural causes, and the ever active, ever working mind having seen things when awake, seems to see them again when asleep? Which is the more philosophical cause, to interpret these phenomena according to the superstitions of old women, or by natural explanations? "

" Dreams are not seldom obscure, with hard interpretations. Surely the gods do not mean to *hide* their meaning from us; or why do they send us any dreams at all? "

" Suppose a medical man were to prescribe to a sick man an earth-born, grass-walking, house-carrying, unsanguineous animal, instead of simply saying, a snail; so Amphion in ' Pacuvius ' speaks of —

> 'A four-footed and slow-going beast,
> Rugged, debased, and harsh; his head is short,
> His neck is serpentine, his aspect stern;
> He has no blood, but is an animal
> Inanimate, not voiceless.'

When these obscure verses had been duly recited, the Greeks cried out, ' We do not understand you unless you tell us plainly what animal you mean? ' ' I mean,' said Pacuvius, ' I mean in one word, a tortoise.' ' Could you not, then,' said the questioner, ' have told us so at first? ' "

Interpreters are not to be relied on; for if they were, they would never differ in opinion — but they constantly do. A runner, the night before the Olympic Games, dreamed that he was driven in a chariot drawn by four horses. He sought out an interpreter, who said, " You will win, as intimated by the strength and swiftness of the horses "; but when he consulted a second interpreter he got the reply, " You will certainly lose, as intimated by the four horses being harnessed in front of you, and therefore attaining the goal before you."

Another competitor in the Games dreamed beforehand of an eagle. " You will win your race," said the first interpreter, "because the eagle is the swiftest of birds." " You will certainly be beaten," said the second, " for an eagle chases and drives other birds, which fly before it, and the eagle is left behind."

On the other hand, there certainly are wonderful tales of dreams that have come true; but what proof have we that they are not concocted for the purpose? And if, as we are told, Alexander once had a wonderful prophetic dream, why is it that he had no others?

And then, what sense is there in the common interpretation that to dream of an egg means a treasure? Surely, the gods would not descend to such paltry joking.

Finally, what is the use of the interpreter's lore, and of dream books? One might dream of anything under the sun, and neither man nor book can foresee and analyze all dreams; in short, there can be no proper science of dreams. The conclusion can only be that divination is absurd, that dreams are natural, and that wise men will pay them no attention whatever.

Cicero's patiently argued opinion does not rest on these arguments alone; it is supported at the present day by many other facts. Nothing is more convincing than the sort of dream, by no means rare, in which operations of the mind, performed when awake, are continued in sleep — the dreamer solves mathematical problems, " meditates the thankless muse," and invents puns and quibbles. We feel that one and the same process goes on in the dream as awake. A case in point is related by Charlotte Brontë.* " I asked her whether she had ever taken opium, as the description given of its effects in ' Villette ' was so exactly like what I had experienced — an exaggerated presence of objects, of which the outlines were indistinct, or lost in golden mist, etc. She replied, that she had never, to her knowledge, taken a grain of it in any shape, but that she had followed the process she always adopted when she had to describe anything which had not fallen within her own experience; she had thought intently on it for many and many a night before falling to sleep — wondering what it was like, or how it would be — till at length, sometimes after the progress of her story had been arrested at this one point for weeks, she awakened in the morning with all clear before her, as if she had in reality gone through the experience, and then could

*" The Life of Charlotte Brontë", Chapter XXVII, by Mrs. Gaskell.

describe it, word for word, as it had happened. I cannot account for this psychologically; I only am sure that it was so, because she said it."

" The Devil's Sonata " of Tartini was composed in a dream. The devil seemed to appear, and play on his violin the sonata that Tartini had been struggling in vain to compose; and next day Tartini transcribed it. Condorce, the mathematician, solved in a dream a difficult problem that had baffled him awake. Condillac often, while reading for his degree, finished off in his dreams the discussions he had entered upon awake. Coleridge, while staying near Porlock in 1797, composed in a dream (not uninfluenced by opium) the most musical and langorous of his poems, " Kubla Khan," based upon a book, " Purchas's Pilgrimage," that he had been reading at the moment of falling asleep.

Innumerable similar phenomena, the truth of which cannot be reasonably doubted, attest the fact that waking processes of mind may continue into our sleep and dreams, the activity of the mind being rather increased than diminished, problems resolving as if by magic, and long-forgotten names spontaneously rising to mind.

The French investigator, Maury, one night had a dream of a town called Mussidan, one of the dream characters averring that it was in the department of the Dordogne. Remembering the dream next day, Maury could not recollect ever having heard of a town of that name, but he found it in a gazeteer, and it *was* in the Dordogne Department. Evidently, at some time or other, long forgotten, he had heard of the place, and his dream had retained and reproduced the memory.

Once a cashier in a Glasgow bank, becoming worried about an error in his books, had a dream in which he saw a man enter the bank, withdraw a small sum from his account, and leave the premises, while he himself, diverted from his duty by a rush of other customers, forgot to enter the transaction, in his books. He recollected the dream next day, and also the transaction, the sum named in the dream being exactly the missing amount, and the error was straightened out.*

A youth, prosecuted for debt, submitted the defence that he had in fact paid it a long time ago. With neither receipt nor witnesses, he apprehended that the case was lost, when he had a vivid dream in which he saw his deceased father, who gave him the name of a witness to the payment. The man was found, and, when he was told certain details of the appearance of the room (as given in the dream) where the business had been transacted, he recollected the affair, and saved the situation.

Quite unimportant things, scarcely noticed when they occur, may come back to mind in this way.

*"Inquiries concerning the Intellectual Powers," by Abercrombie.

A newly married couple (as related by Professor Reubold, of Würzburg), having to clear the dinner table in a hurry, in order to write an important letter, found soon after that a watch, which had been lying on the table, had vanished. They searched high and low for it, without success. A week later, the husband had a dream, in which he put the watch into the outer breast pocket of the coat he had been wearing when the watch disappeared. Next morning, he looked for it again, and found it safe and sound where the dream had shown.

> " Forgotten things long cast behind
> Rush forward in the brain, and come to mind."

Punning in dreams is not rare. Maury dreamed that he went on a Pèlerinage (pilgrimage), met Pelletier (a chemist), and was given a Pelle (shovel). On another occasion, he saw a series of things, the names of which had a resemblance in sound — a *kilometre*, a *kilogramme*, *Gilolo* (an island), lobelia, General *Lopez*, and *Loto* (a game). A friend of Maury's had a dream of the same kind, of the *Jardin* des Plantes; there he saw *Chardin*, the traveler, who gave him a book of Jules *Janin's*.

There are also certain dreams, called by some writers " lucid dreams,"[*] in which we know that we are dreaming and act with a sort of guided

* See art. by Dr. Frederick van Eeden in "Proceedings of the S. P. R." Vol. XXVI, 1912-13, page 41 *et seq.*

will power; but if dreams were conveyed to us by supernatural visitants, this would not be so.

" In general," wrote Lucretius, " as each of us, having pursued any study, is devoted to it in his thoughts . . . we seem, for the most part, to go through the same employment in sleep. Lawyers seem to plead causes, and to make laws; generals to fight and engage in battles; sailors to wage settled war with the winds; and myself to pursue this work, and investigate perpetually the nature of things, and to explain it, when discovered, in the language of my country."

Dreams betray a physical origin also in their susceptibility to physical stimuli, and their sensitiveness to states of the body. " Physicians will tell us," wrote Sir Thomas Browne, " that some food makes us turbulent, some gives quiet dreams. Cato, who doted upon cabbage, might find the cruel effects thereof in his sleep; wherein the Egyptians might find some advantage by their superstitious abstinence from onions. Pythagoras might have calmer sleeps, if he totally abstained from beans."

A dream is reported by Krauss, in which the moon acted as stimulus, perhaps accounting for some of the Roman and Greek moon mythology. Krauss awakened with his arms stretched out towards the window, where his fiancée seemed to be standing. It was the moon —

" But oh! as to embrace me she inclined,
   I waked, she fled, and day brought back my night."

A certain Scherner fell asleep one morning, with the sun shining direct in his eyes, and he had a dream of a fiery dragon approaching him. The dragon came on faster and faster, and then slower and slower, at last stopping dead and making off again, Scherner waking up to find that a heavy cloud was just passing over the face of the sun.

Weygandt, while half asleep on a railway journey, vaguely heard the whistle of the engine, and simultaneously had a dream in which a girl gave a shrill scream. Another dream is reported, in which there was a duel with pistols, occasioned by the dreamer's hearing a door bang and a chain fall on the floor. Also Maury, as a boy, falling asleep one day in the sun, had a dream in which his head lay on an anvil, and a blacksmith was striking it blow after blow with a hammer. His head little by little melted away to water, and he woke up, streaming with perspiration, and heard the clang of the blacksmith's hammer on the anvil in his smithy close by.

Dreams are often influenced by uncomfortable sensations of the body. A counterpane drawn tight against the arm is an embrace, or a heavy weight on the chest; a straw between the toes is impalement on a sharp stake; the clothes slipping off the bed is walking about naked; drops of water falling on the mouth may give a dream of swimming; a silk handkerchief on the nose and mouth of being buried alive; and a mustard plaster on the head, of scalping.

Abercrombie gives some good examples. A certain Doctor Gregory, sleeping with a very hot bottle at his feet, had a dream of walking the crater of Vesuvius barefoot — he had visited Vesuvius in his youth. Abercrombie himself had a dream of winter in Hudson's Bay, in which he suffered severely from the frost, the dream being affected by the chance tossing of his bedclothes off in his sleep, and reading a day or two previous about the state of the Hudson's Bay Territory in winter.

Hunger (as Arctic explorers find) induces dreams of delicious cakes; jaundice, of the world gone yellow; a nasty taste in the mouth, of loathsome foods; and thirst, of dried-up streams, hot deserts, and torrid heat.

Mrs. Radcliffe, the novelist of horrors, took to eating the most indigestible foods in order to procure nightmares for insertion in her tales of horror and mystery. Dryden similarly ate raw flesh to promote dreams of luxurious splendor.

Drugs, also, exert a powerful influence on dreams. Alcohol affects them, but in many different ways; however, if taken in excess, it tends to cause disagreeable dreams, especially of reptiles and vermin (like Bishop Hatto's of rats). Opium dreams are more voluptuous and grandiose; as were De Quincey's: his were of fantastic oriental scenes and tortures, and his sense of space and time were so magnified that buildings and landscapes pained his sight to gaze on, and a single night seemed to stretch out into seventy or a hundred years. Hashish, or Indian hemp, induces horrible nightmares, and sometimes homicidal mania (from which circumstance the word " assassin " is derived from it). The fumes of carbon-bisulphide, impregnating the atmosphere in rubber factories, induce nightmares in which the sleeper leaps over precipices, or is brutally murdered.

All this evidence points to the fact that dreaming has a natural and not a spiritual origin; it appears to work in a regular and uniform way. The way dreams vary with different sorts of people is another fact in support. Dr. Marie de Manacéine collected data, over a period of five years, of the dreams of thirty-seven very different people, and arrived at the following conclusions: the educated and active brained dreamed more than the uneducated and slow; the dreams of the educated were the more logical, complex, and varied (four-fifths of the dreams of the uneducated were mere reproductions of recent waking experience); journalists, chemists, schoolmasters, and other brain workers had only from three to ten dreamless nights a month, whereas manual workers had from eight to twenty-five, and dreams become rarer and rarer with age.

But what above all implies a natural and unmysterious origin of dreams is their content, which is an *ollapodrida* of the impressions of waking life. Detailed analysis of our dreams will show that what we see is compounded of what we have seen — the elements defying detection being what we have in waking life forgotten.

" I believe," says MacNish,* " that dreams are uniformly the resuscitation or re-embodiment of thoughts which have formerly, in some shape or other, occupied the mind. They are old ideas revived, either in an entire state or heterogeneously mingled together. . . .

" I lately dreamed that I walked upon the banks of the Great Canal in the neighborhood of Glasgow. On the side opposite to which I was, and within a few feet of the water, stood the splendid portico of the Royal Exchange. A gentleman whom I knew, was standing upon one of the steps, and we spoke to each other. I then lifted a large stone, and poised it in my hand, when he said that he was certain that I could not throw it to a certain spot which he pointed out. I made the attempt and fell short of the mark. At this

* " The Philosophy of Sleep."

moment a well-known friend came up, whom I knew to excel at putting the stone; but, strange to say, he had lost both his legs, and walked upon wooden substitutes. This struck me as exceedingly curious; for my impression was that he had only lost one leg, and had but a single wooden one. At my desire he took up the stone, and, without difficulty, threw it beyond the point indicated by the gentleman upon the opposite side of the canal.

"The absurdity of this dream is extremely glaring; and yet, on strictly analyzing it, I found it to be wholly composed of ideas, which passed through my mind on the previous day, assuming a new and ridiculous arrangement. I can compare it to nothing but that well-known amusement which consists in putting together a number of sentences, each written on a separate piece of paper, into a hat, shaking the whole, then taking them out one by one as they come, and seeing what kind of medley the heterogeneous compound will make when thus fortuitously put together.

"For instance I had, on the above day, taken a walk to the canal with a friend. On returning from it, I pointed out to him a spot where a new road was forming, and where, a few days before, one of the workmen had been overwhelmed by a quantity of rubbish falling upon him, which fairly chopped off one of his legs, and so much damaged the other that it was feared amputation would be necessary. Near the very spot there is a park, in which, about a month previously, I practiced throwing the stone. On passing the Exchange on my way home, I expressed regret at the lowness of its situation, and remarked what a fine effect the portico would have were it placed upon more elevated ground. Such were the previous circumstances, and let us see how they bear upon the dream.

" In the first place, the canal appeared before me. (2) Its situation is an elevated one. (3) The portico of the Exchange, occurring to my mind as being placed too low, became associated with the elevation of the canal, and I placed it close by on a similar altitude. (4) The gentleman I had been walking with was the same whom, in the dream, I saw standing upon the steps of the portico. (5) Having related to him the story of the man who lost one limb, and had a chance of losing another, this idea brings before me a friend with a brace of wooden legs, who, moreover, appears in connection with putting the stone, as I know him to excel at that exercise. There is only one other element in the dream which the preceding events will not account for, and that is the surprise at the individual referred to having more than one wooden leg. But why should he have even one, seeing that in reality he is limbed like other people? This, also, I can account for. Some years ago, he slightly injured his knee while leaping a ditch, and I remember jocularly advising him to get it cut off. I am particular in illustrating this point with regard to dreams, for I hold that, if it were possible to analyze them all, they would invariably be found to stand in the same relation to the waking state as the above."

If (said Darwin) a man is struck deaf early in life, he has no sounds in his dreams; a man that had been deaf for thirty years, had dreams in which the figures spoke the deaf-and-dumb language, or wrote their words on paper. The blind (according to an article, by Mr. Johns, in the *National Review*, 1885) dream a good deal, mostly of hearing, touch, and smell, and if they are struck blind before they are five years old, they never see at all in their dreams: they realize the dimensions of a room by the sound of footsteps in it; recognize people by their voices or by touch; and feel the freshness of morning by the smell of the air.

There is no escaping the conclusion that dreams are of natural origin and arise from some process, not yet understood, of the brain, but similar in kind to waking processes. Bergson concludes that "our memories are packed away under pressure like steam in a boiler, and the dream is their escape-valve."*

* "Dreams," translated by E. E. Slosson.

But the mystery of dreams is not much nearer solution if we do grant them to be natural products; their exact origin, composition, and elaboration are still conjectural. We have reached the point where they are to be discussed as unconscious cerebration; and no more.

Some of the more obsolete theories may be easily dismissed. One school (to which Hazlitt and Descartes belonged) said that the mind was active asleep just as awake, with continuous dreaming all night through; and that we forgot the multitude of them to remember one or two outstanding ones. They said that, whenever and wherever a sleeper awoke, he always awoke out of a dream, remembered or not, and knew that he had just been dreaming.

Another school claimed (in the words of Pope) that,

" The last image of that troubled heap,
    When sense subsides, and fancy sports in sleep,
    Though past the recollection of the thought,
    Becomes the stuff of which our dream is wrought."

Already indeed in the fourth century before Christ, Aristotle had attributed dreams to the impressions objects left on the mind, but they were exaggerated in the memory, and a slight sound became a clap of thunder.

A great impetus was given in modern times to this way of thinking, by Henri Bergson's paper, read to the French Institut Psychologique on March 26, 1901, on the possibility of exploring the unconscious workings of the brain through the channel of dreams. In it, Bergson said that if we closed our eyes, and gazed attentively as if they were still open, we should first see a black background, and then transient points of light, moving up and down, and changing size very slowly, some one color, some another, brilliant or dull according to the person, and colliding with or displacing one another. They are caused by slight changes in the circulation of the blood in the retina, or by the closed eyelid pressing on the eye and exciting the optic nerve; and are called variously "ocular spectra," "colored spots," and "phosphenes."

At the moment of falling off to sleep, we see the colored spots join together and begin to resemble the images of our dreams. According to Professor Ladd, when we wake up we may see the dream figures melt away again into the colored spots; a newspaper melts into a white spot sprinkled with black; the sea, with yeasty waves and snowy foam, melts into a spot half yellow and half gray, shot with tiny points of light.

Given the colored spots, and varieties of stimuli inside the body and out of it, imagination does the rest. The buzzings in our ears, that awake we sometimes hear, sound louder in sleep, and resemble the murmur of voices. Smell, taste and touch are as easily affected; and so the process of dreaming is complete.

The partially clothed dream would be explained in some such way as this: while we are asleep, some of the bedclothes slip off, or the massing of the clothes is shifted, and a train of thoughts connected with nakedness is started; meanwhile the colored spots assume the shape of a familiar room or street, and we discover ourselves passing through it scantily clothed, yet exciting no surprise in the beholders. (In his novel, " Before Adam," Jack London ingeniously ascribed this dream to hereditary influences. As our ancestors went naked, a desire for that state became perpetuated in the race, but was prevented from fulfilment in ordinary life by a prohibitive social sense, and could satisfy its object only in the non-restrictive world of imagination. It is common amongst madmen to want to run through the streets naked.)

The falling dream is similarly explained. In sleep, as we are prone in bed, our feet, accustomed all day to the resistance of the ground, have a different feeling, which we tend, in moments of forgetfulness, to interpret as that of standing in mid-air, and falling through space. (Jack London has an explanation for this, too. The falling dream is derived from the age when prehistoric man lived in trees. Withered branches or imperfect grasp caused many headlong tumbles to the ground; if no intercepting branch broke the fall, the ape-man died and left no offspring — and so we never dream of reaching the ground, — but wake up — as we are in the line of descent of those that fell, but escaped with nothing worse than a violent shock, being saved by lower branches, or some other timely obstacle.)

Bergson attempts to develop his theory, in order to account for the many well-known properties of dreams. Ocular spectra, he argues, are idealized into the images of our dreams by the creative power of our imagination, which, in its turn, depends upon our memory. During the day, memory is steeped in the present, in our impressions of actions, feelings, environment; we are, as it were, partial to the passing moment; during sleep, on the other hand, memory is impartial, it does not discriminate between impressions of ten years ago and impressions of the day, past and present mingling in perfect freedom. Throngs of memories of all kinds, recent and remote, pleasant and unpleasant, strive against one another for the privilege of rising to the surface, but only those succeed that bear a strong resemblance to the colored spots in our eyes, the internal and external stimuli of the body at the moment, and the general tone of our health, mentality and sensibility. Then the dream is generated.

The process of dreaming now closely resembles that of seeing (Bergson expediently ignores hearing, smelling and other experiences common in dreams — one cannot be expected to hear or smell these so-called ocular spectra), and depends upon similar laws. In looking at a landscape we do not behold at once each particular detail, but take the details for granted, and see a modified outline of the outstanding features; in reading, except in infancy when learning, we do not see each separate letter in a word, but a whole sign which we interpret automatically, and our imagination supplies the rest. We are deceived by an illusion of the senses into the belief that we see every detail of the landscape and of the word, but it is not actually so; the process is divinatory. Likewise in dreaming, the colored spots furnish an outline or sketchy shape, and that is all we ever actually see, but imagination supplying a host of details, we suppose next day that we have seen a multitude of things, and are permanently deceived. In point of fact, the story of a dream is composed after the dream is over — and in this observation Bergson has really hit upon the truth, however mistaken are the rest of his contentions.

We are, Bergson continues, during all the waking hours, continually in a state of tension, arising from the process of adapting ourselves to our environment, and so, while we clearly perceive the outstanding things round about us, we are blind to many others that penetrate our minds and leave their impress all unknown to our conscious selves. In sleep, unremarked impressions of this kind, now that the state of tension is no more, assume an equal importance with the conscious impressions, and in the sequel our sense of proportion is quite lost. " The dream," to quote Bergson, " consists of the entire mental life, minus the tension, the effort, and the bodily movement. We perceive still, we remember still, we reason still. . . . What requires an effort is the precision of adjustment. . . . It is this force that the dreamer lacks." On that account dreams are incoherent and unregulated: a green spot speckled with white points would answer just as well for a lawn bespangled with daisies, or a billiard table dotted with balls. Logicality falls to pieces: incidents that we have been most moved at in witnessing appear in juxtaposition, though they have no connection of time, person, place or idea. More, the time sense is lost; for there is no social round by which time can be portioned out.

Such is Bergson's not very satisfactory or convincing theory; and it is typical of a number of theories formulated on the supposition of unconscious cerebration. Mr. Havelock Ellis advances another.* He divides dreams, as do Sully, Foucault

* " The World of Dreams," 1911.

and Tissié also, into two categories, namely, dreams resulting from direct bodily sensations, or presentative dreams, and dreams resulting from thoughts and memories or representative dreams. As presentative dreams do not literally repeat our sensations, there is some invention in them, too, and they are in that degree " representative "; but the representative dream proper is without any perceptible bodily stimulus.

Word-play dreams (which are representative) afford him what he considers a clue to the real nature of mental processes in sleep. As objects are dubbed by wrong names, sentences twisted into the wrong order, and puns made (*e.g.* Hall and Hell), he assumes that the brain can think and reason in sleep; therefore, as we undoubtedly translate sensations, also into dream images, must not dreaming be the product of an unceasing reasoning process, the function of which is to harmonize, in the period when our brain is off active duty, the limited and incongruous data offered to the senses during sleep? Dreams are, he says, " to supply adequate theories to account for the magnified emotional impulses borne in upon our sleeping consciousness. Sleeping consciousness is assailed by waves of emotion from various parts of the organism, but is entirely unable to detect their origin, and, therefore, invents an explanation of them. . . . The fundamental source of our dream life may thus be said to be emotion."

But this theory offers no explanation why one dream should differ from another, when the bodily state is the same; it affords no explanation of the infinite variety of dreams. Why should we dream about mice, ladders, swimming baths? What have *they* to do with the interpretation of sensation and emotions?

Still less satisfying is the observation and theorizing of lesser men. Dr. Frederick van Eeden* advances wild theories that are unworthy either the rational arguments of the modern scientific school or the poetical superstition of the past, though he treads in both paths himself. He invents categories of dreams that exist nowhere but in his own imagination. He states that the initial dream, which occurs at the beginning of sleep, when the body is just healthily tired, imparts the sensation of floating and flying, and arises independent of the stimulus of bodily sensation. This is mere supposition, unsupported by observation. "Very vivid dreams," he goes on to say, " are rare, and may occur at any stage of sleep. Symbolic dreams are mocking and painful, erotic and lewd; what is more, they are sent into our minds by demons, to torment us . . . ."

* " A Study of Dreams," in Proceedings of the S. P. R., Vol. XXVI 1912–1913, p. 431, *et seq.*

General dreams (how precise and recognizable the categories are) are of rare occurrence, and belong to the middle of the night only! In lucid dreams, we dream that we are dreaming, and possess a semi-conscious control of our behavior; such dreams occur between the hours of five and eight in the morning. " There is a saying by the German poet, Novalis, that when we dream that we dream, we are near waking up. This view I reject. Lucid dreams occur in deep sleep, and do not as a rule end in waking up, unless I wish it and do it by an act of volition." In demon dreams, which are borne in upon us by enemy demons, we see demons gesticulating and acting besides in a manner intended to scare us. Other demons send us wrong waking-up dreams, in which we think to awaken in our bedroom, but find ourselves still asleep! Finally, there is the pathological dream, which is a common variety, and is brought about through the influence of indigestion, fever, poisoning, or other discomfort; they may occur at any time of the night, but our memories of them next day are untrustworthy.

This magnificent theorizing is typical of a good deal thrust upon us by credulous mediocrities dabbling in this difficult subject. But even Bergson's and Mr. Havelock Ellis' theories, more logical, plausible, and in keeping with physical law, carry us very little farther. They are too mechanical and obvious by half. There is nothing inevitable or convincing about them, nothing of that recognizable but undefinable quality of finality of the theories that have long carried weight, like the theory of gravitation (only now threatened by Einstein's Theory). Superstition is objectionable because it is superstition; but scientific hypotheses, even though wrong, are not disagreeable, because there is sure to be some element of truth in them, when formulated by intelligent minds, and a gradual development may proceed till the true theory is at last reached. There is something more in dreaming than mere continuance of waking thought, or than mere colored spots in the eyes happening to conjure up vivid pictures in the imagination; but both ideas offer scope for further investigation and development, and so their formulation is a milestone on the road to final knowledge. There is an unanalyzable, magic element in dreams that these theories do not touch, but that looms large in the old superstitions; and the truth about dreams will be obtained when this magic element — connected somehow with the personality of the sleeper, and his fortunes — is brought into contact with the rational element, — as in the work of the medical investigators of the present day, who are immensely aided in their task by constant practical experience of dreams, dreamers and life.

Unconscious cerebration, then, is not an arid formula, but a step on the pleasant road of truth; and Claudian was making no unimportant observation when he wrote:

> " Day thoughts, transwinged from th' industrious breast,
> All seem re-acted in the night's dumb rest.
> When the tired Huntsman, his repose begins,
> Then flies his mind to woods, and wild beast dens,
> Judges dream cases: Champions seem to run,
> With their night-Coursers, the vain hounds to shun
> Love hugs his rapes, the Merchant traffic minds.
> The miser thinks he some lost treasure finds.
> And to the thirsty sick, some potion cold,
> Stiff flattering sleep, inanely seems to hold.
> Yea, and in th' age of silent rest, even I,
> Troubled with Art's deep musings, nightly lie."

Life and dreams cannot be separated. Napoleon when he was in danger of his life from the explosion of the infernal machine fired by St. Regent in the Rue St. Nicaise, lay dreaming in his carriage " of the danger I had undergone some years before in crossing the Tagliamento at midnight by the light of torches, during a flood."[*] Apprehension had generated an apprehensive dream. There is some truth in the superstitious view of dreams; there is some in that of unconscious cerebration: they only want blending.

---

[*] See Lockhart's " Life of Napoleon Buonaparte," Chap. XV.

CHAPTER VII

DREAMS AS WISH FULFILMENTS

"I believe it to be true that Dreams are the true Interpreters of our inclinations; but there is an Art required to sort and understand them." — *Montaigne*, "Essais," III, 13.

"On analytical investigation, it becomes plain that the dream, as we remember it, is only a façade which conceals the contents within the house." — *Jung*, "New Paths in Psychology."

SOME fifty years ago, the Darwinian theory that arouses scarce a scientific comment today, was fiercely disputed, and accounted gross heresy. The theories of Dr. Freud of Vienna are in the same plight today; but it is certain that, however much they have to be modified in the future, a substantial part of them must always stand as true and basic in relation to the operations of the mind.

The theory of consciousness has had a Crusoe-like development.* At first the Crusoe conscious had no doubt that the island of consciousness really *was* an island, or that the rational Robinson Crusoe was its only inhabitant. Then the suspicion arose in his mind that the island was really a peninsula, with a low-lying isthmus alternately covered or exposed with the flow and ebb of the

* Dr. James Olivier, in an address to the Society for the Study of Orthophysics, June, 1919.

tide, while the main land was a misty continent of " subconsciousness." The third stage was entered upon when he found footprints on the shore, pointing to the mainland; and this was when, some twenty years ago, Dr. Sigmund Freud, of Vienna, " discovered definite traces of a persistent and active mode of mental functioning, alien, unacceptable, and above all imperceptible to the rational mind." Man contained an unknown within himself, the existence of whom had never before been suspected. As Darwin had contended that man's " bodily structure concealed compromising evidence of lowly origin in the shape of remnants of older structures," so Freud contended that " somewhere in the depths of his personality lurked primitive tendencies, which bore as little relation to his present-day needs as his gill-clefts, but which had, all unknown to him, a very large say in shaping his conduct."

In short, from the study of dreams, Dr. Freud drew the conclusion that our minds have depths beyond what we ourselves realize, but which by certain means can be investigated; and that the hidden activities of these depths bear a powerful influence, all unknown to ourselves, upon our conduct and feelings. This inner mind is called by him the *unconscious*.

From the study of normal dreams, Dr. Freud might never have made his discovery; but as a neurologist, having to deal with every kind of nervous derangement, many of which are accompanied by extraordinary dreams, he was led to a solution of the mystery, and the formulation of theories applicable to every kind of dream. His deepest interest was in cases of arrested development; and he soon drew the conclusion that some of the cases had been caused by forgotten, but none the less havoc-working, memories. The patients were hypnotized, and questioned; but the answers not proving as satisfactory as he wished, he developed another and better method of reaching the patients' forgotten memories, namely, that of " free-association." Starting on some familiar idea, like that of home life, he questioned the patient in his conscious state on all the thoughts he had that bore on it; then, one idea leading on to another, he pressed the inquiry till he could get no further. The patient would fail to answer, and he knew then that at last he had traced the idea about which clung the patient's painful memory, covered up by an accumulation of other memories. This method proved fairly successful, except when the memories went too far back in infancy, or were otherwise thickly overlaid.

What results he did obtain pointed uniformly in the same direction, namely, to early childhood as the period when dangerous memories were formed, and that these memories, though forgotten, exerted incalculable indirect influence upon the patient. He therefore began the study of the infant mind and its tendencies, which he found different in kind from the adult's, but akin to those of primitive man. Evidence came to light showing that a child of, say, six months of age, is actuated by powerful motives — not, of course, conscious — and that these motives, though later suppressed, exert a preponderating influence, during the whole of lifetime, over its personality and conduct.

The name unconscious was applied to these motives for obvious reasons; for, though the unconscious finds an outlet in adults, and though its influence on thought and action is easy to observe, it so disguises its real nature, and deceives the onlooker, who is not warned of its elusive devices, that in all the history of mankind no one has been specifically aware of it — men have realized it, but never isolated its characteristics and its functions. " The unconscious is inaccessible to direct introspection." The universal realization of unconscious tendencies is reflected in the popular expressions, " the old Adam in us," " getting one's monkey up," " possessed by the devil "; but only today are we able to investigate the unconscious scientifically.

A host of questions rush to our mind at once

when we tackle this problem. How, for instance, could Freud explore this new world, divided from consciousness by so formidable a barrier of disguise and dissimulation? How *could* we be unconscious of tendencies so powerful and universal? What was their method of disguise, and what was the mechanism that produced it? All these questions have been, whether satisfactorily or not, answered in detail by Freud and his school.

The child, according to Freud's ideas, is born with a well-developed unconscious (a sort of bundle of strong instincts), but little conscious. However, as the child cannot speak, and has no conscious memory, it has hitherto remained an inscrutable mystery what his unconscious was like; for when language, memory, and the conscious are developed, the unconscious suffers eclipse, and is totally excluded from the child's waking thought. However, later on in life, should any derangement of the nervous system take place, the unconscious recovers some degree of its infantile ascendency; and then the physician can gather some idea of its nature.

The unconscious, Freud finds, is veritably the Old Adam in us all: " Its aims are almost grotesquely at variance with those of the cultured social self, and are shut out from consciousness by a vigorous subliminal mechanism called the censor, which is not a permanent official armed with a blue pencil, but merely the expression of a violent incompatibility between an older and more recent level of mental functioning. As a result of this conflict, the primitive conative trend, or wish, must camouflage itself to an extent varying with the cultural status of the individual."

The unconscious is thus a sort of primitive man in us, unrepressed by any moral code or by any conscience, determined to defend its existence to the last: it prompts us to eat and drink, to love and hate, without regard to the rights or feelings of others, it is selfish and sensual, and consists of wishes that are more and more opposed to the conscious as the latter is higher and higher developed.

The all-powerful unconscious of the child is soon checked and brought under control. The unconscious impels the child to cry for the moon, but stern necessity forbidding satisfaction of the desire, disappointment ensues. Earth has limits beyond which it cannot satisfy the unbounded cravings of the unconscious; and so has man. Baby wants to eat brother Jack's finger, but the unwillingness of brother Jack to have any part of his person eaten, again brings in the sequel of disappointment, and so the counter-wishes of other human beings begin to operate against the unconscious. Still greater in its influence is the social atmosphere round the child, encouraging certain actions, discouraging others, according to the sanction of the herd; the unconscious is again balked, the child is constrained to do as others do; and at last the conscious is lord and master of the unconscious, to the satisfaction and the interest of the human family. The unconscious becomes " the *abandoned* psychic life of the child."

One is led, then, by Freud, to reject the old theory that a child is born with a mind blank like a sheet of white paper,* unbiased and innocent, and destined to become exactly what environment, education, and religious teaching make it. Far from that being true, the child is born with the original sin of the unconscious, and the limited free will of the conscious. People may think to prevent terrors from possessing the minds of the young by keeping tales of bogies and horrors away from them, and, of course, it is a wise thing to do: but despite that protection, many children will still be a prey to terrors of the night, as these will arise, independent of experience, from their lurking place in the unconscious.

Amongst the various cravings of the unconscious, Freud lays special stress (more than other investigators) on one, as the most powerful at the time, and the most potent in future effect — namely, the sexual, or love craving. Above the desire for drink and food and air stands the desire

* Locke, " Essay on the Human Understanding."

for affection, which at this stage of life is directed towards the parents, towards the father especially if the child is a girl, and if the child is a boy, then towards the mother. As a complement to this, the child feels repulsion, out of jealousy, for the parent of its own sex. Later, it represses this feeling, with the result that (to " let off steam " as it were) dreams are generated, often of the death of the parent disliked; but if the repression is not complete, nervous troubles may occur in later life as a direct consequence. This repression is called the Œdipus Complex, after King Œdipus of Thebes, who in ignorance who she was married his own mother, Jocasta, and finally, guiltless though he was in intent, paid for the unholy deed with his life.

The irresolution of mind that plagues Hamlet, and causes him again and again to delay taking revenge on his uncle, Claudius, who has married Hamlet's widowed mother, would be attributed by Freud to the Œdipus Complex. Hamlet cannot freely will his uncle's death, for the murder of his father, because he had himself in childhood desired his father's death; the wish had been sternly repressed, he is quite ignorant of its existence but it ferments still in his unconscious, and imposes a fatal check upon his will. If Hamlet had even suspected that once he had himself wished for his father's death, he would have been deeply grieved; and to dream of killing him, or seeing him killed, would have been painful. The censor, therefore, is kind to Hamlet in keeping such thoughts rigidly out of his mind; and making even dreams of his father's death be so disguised that Hamlet would not realize what they were about.

We have seen how in infancy the conscious gradually obtains the supremacy over the unconscious. In the adult brain, there is, as it were, still another level of mental activity — that of the foreconscious. The highest level, or conscious, consists of the thoughts, feelings, and desires uppermost in my mind at this moment; the next level, or foreconscious, consists of the thoughts, feelings and wishes latent in my mind (*i.e.* I can call them up before me at will), but which I am not concerned with at the moment; last, and lowest level, is the unconscious, which consists of the repressed desires of early infancy.

It is through his conscious that the reader is aware of these remarks; it is in his foreconscious that all the facts learned, feelings experienced, and desires formed, during his lifetime, are stored; it is by his unconscious that his personality is fixed, and his satisfaction in life realized.

The censor is stationed midway between the unconscious and the foreconscious — like Michael between Hades and Paradise — and it is his charge to oppose any attempt on the part of the unconscious to send any wishes up to the foreconscious. Between the latter, however, and the conscious there is no obstacle to passing, and so any thought in the foreconscious, provided the field of attention and the intensity are favorable, may pass up to the conscious. Thus, suppose that a desire to be in one's mother's arms (a quite common desire) lurks in the unconscious, it will try to force its way up to the foreconscious level, and would succeed in doing so were it not for the vigilant censor — vigilant, *i.e.* except in sleep — who promptly bans it. On the other hand if a thought of the approach of teatime tries to rise from the foreconscious to the conscious, it will pass into it as soon as the conscious has leisure to pay it attention.

Dreams are caused by wishes, according to Freud; not wishes in the conscious, for by themselves they are seldom intense enough to produce a dream; but unconscious infantile wishes, which possess a great store of energy, and can utilize it to reinforce a conscious wish that has some association of ideas with them. The dream is then an imaginary fulfilment of the wish, relieving the mind, and soothing the nervous sytem. (The only wish that is common to all dreams, and that comes from the foreconscious, is that to continue sleeping; which is probably an infantile wish that

has never been repressed, and so never consigned
to the unconscious.) The unconscious wishes are
selfish; and the dreams are egoistic, for if the
dreamer does not appear imaged in his own
person, he is present as something or somebody
else.

The mind, or "psyche," therefore, is more
than mere waking consciousness: it is a triple
mechanism; and the conscious is, as it were, the
observing and reporting organ for the other two
divisions. The most important division is the
unconscious, which is also the one we are least
aware of, and most ignorant about; but its desires
obtain fulfilment only in disguised ways, as, for
instance, in the form of the dream. A dream is
the result of a complex process, called the dream
work, which is, for purposes of description, divis-
ible into several parts; and the first of them is
condensation.

This process starts in the unconscious: certain
desires fermenting there — "nothing but a wish
can impel our psychic apparatus to activity" —
begin to take a definite course. Let us suppose
that ten of them want to ascend to the foreconscious. They dare not make the attempt as they
are in their own shape, with the censor ever ready
to intercept them and drive them back; they must
look about for some disguise, and not attempt to
appear in dreams in their own persons.

The strongest of the ten wishes take the lead, link up with any others that have something in common with them, and neglect the rest, who then abandon the enterprise. A sort of précis of the ten wishes is the result. The compression is absolute: thoughts and emotions of fifty years apart may be expressed by one and the same single image or group of images; thus ten public examinations that had been feared (a *wish* that they should *not* take place) may be represented for the purposes of dreaming by the face of the one-eyed invigilator at one of the examinations, or by a clock-face with the minute-hand marking the time to hand in papers: but this is to anticipate. The rival wishes are now *condensed*.

Suppose our ten wishes in the unconscious have been condensed into three, of which one is outstandingly important; then still more to puzzle the censor, the unimportant ones take on increased intensity, and the important one diminishes to a corresponding extent. This process is called *displacement*. It is a " transvaluation of value," or shifting of psychic intensity; the supreme desire, forming the strongest motive of the dream, and presumably to be the central image of the dream, is ordained to appear as some insignificant scrap of scenery, and so enable the condensed wishes to elude the eagle eye of the censor. Suppose that the chief wish was to see Miss ——

soon; then, in the resulting dream, she may appear as the carrier on a motor-cycle, or the press of a tennis racket — for the last time the dreamer saw her, she was sitting on the one, and tightening up the other.

Our three *condensed* and *displaced* wishes have next to be given a concrete form of expression. This is generally not one of words, but of pictures. As one might represent a cow, in a drawing to be shown to a Kaffir who knew no English, by a pair of horns, one's dream thoughts are represented by a visual symbol. It is a natural and universal process. When we say a man is " as brave as a lion," we are offering the hearer a picture of a lion to stand for the abstract idea, " bravery." " He spied three sails in the offing," presents a picture of sails to represent the idea of ships. Slang and proverbial sayings both depend upon the principle of symbolism. " Tophole " is a symbol for " splendid," a " stitch in time saves nine " is a simple coupling of images to represent a complex idea. Symbolism is concise and vivid. And innumerable words and expressions in every language, though they no longer appear symbolical, will prove on examination to have originated that way; thus, " elucidate " goes back to the idea of light, and means " to shed light upon a subject"; but this symbolic picture has been crystallized into a mere sign.

It is, indeed, often a puzzling task, to trace back from a symbol to the original idea that it expressed, if that be in any degree complicated. Were we to dream of holding a bird, and seeing two more sitting in a tree, we should probably be long in grasping its significance, namely that a bird in the hand is worth two in the bush. Or if in a dream we saw two hares running away, yet felt powerless to give chase, it would hardly dawn upon us that the meaning was that of the Japanese proverb, " He who hunts two hares leaves one and loses t'other." Yet in one respect at least that *is* the way to interpret our dreams.

As for slang and Americanisms, consider the following extract from an American novel: " Sir, he's tickled to death and that's a fact. I'm the only one to make a kick, I kind of reckoned on being allowed to play a walking-on part in the drama, but I look like being cut out in the new shuffle." This is all symbolical. A dream is similar, and would appear something like this: " I saw a man, convulsed with laughter, lying on the floor. Somebody was tickling him. He seemed to die. I found myself taking a kick at him. He was quite dead. Then the scene changed. I was in a large theatre in the wings, about to go on the stage. I had no part and could not think what I had to say. Some people were at a card table nearby and I joined in. I picked out a card. It was the king of hearts, and the others drew lower cards. They began to play, and left me out."

The meaning would be that the dreamer desired a certain office or pleasure, of which he looked like being balked.

To return to our three condensed and displaced dream wishes: in some symbolic way, they will be given concrete expression, ready to appear before the mind's eye as a dream. All the images may appear at once, or they may appear in a series, depending upon their associations. If two of the wishes were originally connected, they would appear in symbolic form, together — thus a dream of a picture hanging in the Queen's Hall may represent the two wishes, first to hear a concert, second to visit an art gallery. If one wish was the original cause of the other, they would appear in symbolic form consecutively (sometimes in reverse order, further to elude the censor); and if the wishes were similar in many respects, they would appear either as a single symbol, or as a composite one.

Different symbols serve the same purpose for different people; there is no fixed system, by which to form or to read all dreams, as if a lamb always signified a desire for meat, or a cocoanut a desire to go to a fair. The haphazard associations of experience, and the chance similarity of two words conveying different notions, decide most of them. However, as some experiences are universal, some symbols are common, and express a common desire: desire for a birth is often expressed by the picture of a child entering the water, and a love desire by such symbols as shoes or hats walking upstairs and down, flying through the air, or travelling in some vehicle. The symbols may, however, be much more direct; for example, a patient of Dr. Freud's had dreamed she saw her fifteen-year-old daughter (alive at the time) lying dead in a box — the origin was that, fifteen years before, the mother had hoped that the child would be born dead. Recent memories are generally drawn upon for illustrative purposes, and unimportant ones rather than not; the day before the dream, called the " dream day," is always represented by some experience used as a symbol, and childhood furnishes many other symbols. Unimportant experiences are suitable because they carry no emotional weight with them, and will not deflect the energy released from the unconscious desires; they are also best fitted for the first condition of survival, that of eluding the censor. Some parts of a dream may also symbolize the desire for escape from bodily discomforts arising during the dream process; but if the discomfort is intense, we recognize it consciously, and waken up.

The material, or manifest content, of the dream

is thus a symbolical expression of the condensed and displaced dream wishes that arise from the unconscious, and seek an imaginative outlet in sleep, *i. e.*, while the censor is least watchful; it is also, by reason of the source of the symbols, a collection of images in the memory, taken from experiences of waking life, and connected together by quite superficial associations. The process of symbolization is named, the third in the complete dream work, *dramatization*.

The three processes described so far take place in the sleeping state; the fourth, and final, process takes place, little though we are aware of it, after awakening. It is so momentary, and instinctive, that we think it occurs during sleep; yet it is a complex process, most ingeniously devised both to yield us more satisfaction, and to baffle the censor: it is the process that weaves the chaotic symbols supplied by the first part of the dream work into the tissue of a dream.

In short, after the symbols have been presented to the mind as a mere dumb show, we reconstruct them, make additions, and form them into a consecutive acted drama. This, the last process, is called *secondary elaboration*. It is the result of the censor's action; the content of the dream is given a lively sensible coloring of reality, in order to render it still less like the original dream thoughts, and so still more difficult to recognize for what it is — the expression of unconscious wishes.

Suppose that the dramatization of anxiety (*i.e.*, a negative wish) about some one out of harmony with his surroundings were an image of a billard table with a tea-cup for the red, and a pistol (to stand for our fear for his safety); then in secondary elaboration, the dream might appear in story form as follows: We were playing at billiards, and each time we wished to cannon off the red, we were frustrated by its turning into a tea-cup; at last, as we were falling into a state of despair, a burglar entered and covered us with a pistol; he then fired point blank, and we woke up with a start. Such a dream would effectually screen from our detection the original wish from which it had sprung.

Thus, what we next day call our dream (if the censor has not succeeded in making us forget it altogether, as he usually does) is only the *secondary* elaboration, made by ourselves, of the dramatized form of our desires. However, the camouflage system described above breaks down when the stimulus (*i. e.*, the inspiring and motive wish) is overpowering, and the dream is then a literal expression of the thoughts — *i. e.*, most often a recapitulation of violent experiences passed through. Thus, war patients often dream of battle; as Shakespeare made Mercutio say —

" Sometimes she (*i.e.*, Queen Mab, the bringer of dreams)
  driveth o'er a soldier's neck,
And then dreams he of cutting foreign throats,
Of breaches, ambuscadoes, Spanish blades,
Of healths five fathoms deep; and then anon
Drums in his ear, at which he starts, and wakes,
And being thus frightened, swears a pray'r or two,
And sleeps again"; and also Lady Hotspur,—
" Why hast thou lost the fresh blood in thy cheeks?
In thy faint slumbers . . . thou hast talk'd
Of sallies and retires, of trenches, tents,
Of palisadoes, frontiers, parapets,
Of basilisks, of cannon, culverin,
Of prisoners' ransom, and of soldiers slain,
And all the currents of a heady fight."

The continuous motivity of the shell-shocked causes persistent terrifying dreams, expressing the contemplative fear which fills the unconscious. During the day the patient's attention is diverted from horror by surrounding activities, and there is no dreaming; but during sleep, the mind reverts to scenes of battle, the dreamer screams aloud, issues orders to his men, and lives the old experience all over again. The dream may be forgotten next morning but a cold sweat and a fit of depression tell their tale, and virtue has gone out of the man as much as if he had felt the excitement of an actual fight with bomb, bayonet, rifle and cannon.

Even normal people, when their desires are not in violent conflict with their moral and social convictions, may have undisguised fulfilment dreams; and this is specially so with young children. The desires denied them during the day are granted in imagination during the night. An illustration of this occurs in the autobiography of the Provençal poet, Mistral.* The incident happened when he was about four years old. He had seen for some days that the water-iris in the draw-well moat was beginning to open, and his " hands tingled to pluck some of the lovely golden buds." Arrived at the stream, he climbed down to the water's edge, and stretched out his hand to clutch the flower, when he slipped up to his neck in the water. Soundly rated by his mother, he nevertheless soon found himself at the moat side again, and splash! — the former process was repeated. He was saved by his mother, who soundly rated him as before, and dressed him up in his festal suit. As luck would have it, before long he was beside the moat for the third time, and caution was flung to the winds when the temptation was repeated.

" There were those golden flowers again mirrored in the water and exciting my desire; but a desire so passionate, delirious, excessive, as to make me forget my two previous disasters." He stretched out his hand as before, the reed he clung to with the other hand snapped off short, and for the third time he was in the middle of the stream,

* " Memoirs of Mistral."

head foremost. There was a great fuss made, but he was saved, given a dose of medicine, and put to bed.

" Worn out with emotion, I soon fell asleep. Can any one guess of what I dreamed? Why, of my iris flowers! . . . In a lovely stream of water which wound all round the farmhouse, a limpid, transparent, azure stream like the waters of the fountain at Vaucluse, I beheld the most beautiful clumps of iris covered with a perfect wonder of golden blossoms! Little dragon-flies with blue silk wings came and settled on the flowers, while I swam about naked in the laughing rivulet and plucked by handfuls and armsful those enchanting yellow blooms. And the more I picked the more sprang up. All at once I heard a voice calling me, ' Frédéric! ' I awoke and to my joy I saw a great bunch of golden iris shining by my side. The master himself, my worshipful sire, had actually gone to pick those flowers I so longed for and the mistress, my dear sweet mother, had placed them on my bed."

But this is not the rule, it is the exception. Let us suppose, in the vein of Addison that a common dream becomes a self-conscious personality, endowed with memory and speech, and that it agrees to relate for our edification the history of its life. It might do so in some such form as the following:

" I am a dream, dreamed by a quite ordinary human being, and I was born no longer ago than yesterday. My master, you must know, chancing to catch a glimpse in the street of a girl whose beauty put him strongly in mind of an old sweetheart of his, felt a sudden thrill of pleasure at sight of her; and the train of memories to which the incident had set a spark continued more or less alight till bedtime. These memories were my mother, who was engendered in my master's brain; but she was by herself only a feeble and inactive creature.

" However, to continue my story, my mother spied during the night, to her great surprise, an old friend of hers, Mr. Love-in-early-infancy, immured some distance below her, in my master's state prison, the unconscious; and he told her very shortly how he had been unjustly caged up there almost since my master's first coming into his estate, at about a year old, or a little more. Mother had no sooner heard this, than she communicated her wishes to him, and, finding him mightily sympathetic, made a desperate attempt to reach him and get married to him, despite a terrible Cerberus, called censor, that guarded the passage before the prison, and kept a constant watch upon all egress and ingress. Shortly after, she gave birth to a child, who am I; but I so closely resembled my father in appearance, that she hardly dared hope to get me safe out of prison, the censor knowing my father well by sight.

" After some discussion, it was decided that I should be cunningly disguised, so that neither the censor, nor my mother's strict master, the conscious, should recognize me. First, for I was of extraordinary fatness, the flabby superfluous parts of my body were cut away, by a delicate surgical operation; then my head became swollen as large as my body, by a process seemingly magical, and my body in its turn dwindled away to the former size of my head; and finally, I was presented with a magic nightcap, by virtue of which I appeared to strangers as a picture of a pair of ballroom slippers worn many years ago by the former sweetheart of Mr. Conscious.

" Thus equipped, I went out of the prison in fear and trembling to face the redoubtable censor, as he stood on guard at the gate; and scarce daring to hope that I should make the ascent unhindered to the safe stronghold of the fore-conscious. He examined me with some laxness, methought, for I was not stopped, and I slipped stealthily past him, making all haste to reach my goal, and present my compliments to Mr. Conscious.

" He seemed mightily surprised to see me, and veritably thought (how I laughed up my sleeve) that I *was* a pair of dancing slippers, no more, no less. It *was* a joke, indeed, and I shall never forget it.

" Then events followed one after another in rapid succession. Mr. Conscious began to awaken out of his lethargy, and become dimly aware that a *slipper* and I were two different things. Censor, who now realized that he had been remiss in letting me pass, rushed forward, often stumbling, to prevent Mr. Conscious from understanding my real character; and, in the twinkling of an eye he had told him some cock-and-bull story of a ballroom, a once-popular waltz, and a number of pairs of dancing slippers circling the floor rhythmically, without any human accompaniment. Mr. Conscious, I regret to say, had no suspicion of the deception practiced upon him. He little suspected that I was the child of Love-in-early-infancy, or even of Seeing-an-old-sweetheart; and, indeed, through censor's hypnotic influence, it was not above a minute after, that he had forgotten ever to have seen me at all. And so I died, and was buried in eternal oblivion.

" Such is my tale, and so have I been robbed of my inheritance as a useful member of the community; and here I lie, in the long purgatory of forgotten memories, protesting against the scurvy usage that I have received, and calling down all the plagues and scourges to which mankind is subject upon the villainous censor, and my gullible master, Mr. Conscious. But I have one comfort: my father, Love-in-early-infancy, is much happier in his wearisome prison now that I have escaped from it, and feels in some degree that he himself has enjoyed a moment's sweet freedom in my humble person. May he long flourish! "

.　.　.　.　.　.　.

Such is what the Freudian theory supposes to be the genesis of a dream; and it will be seen, therefore, why great importance is attached to dream analysis at the present day in dealing with nerve patients. Powerful unconscious desires, not effectually under control, will wreck the nerves, *i.e.*, cause a nervous breakdown; and before that breakdown can be intelligently treated, the desires that caused it must be known, as through dreams they generally can be.

Freud has demonstrated and systematized his theory. Others before him had caught glimpses of the truth, as, for instance, Montaigne, in the words at the head of this chapter. MacNish also, in 1834, wrote that " when a person has a strong desire to see any place or object which he has never seen before, he is apt to dream about it; while, as soon as his desire is gratified, he often ceases to dream. I remember hearing a great deal of the beauty of Rouen Cathedral, and in one form or other it was constantly presented before my imagination in dreams; but having at last seen the cathedral I never again dreamed about it. This is not the invariable result of the gratified wish; but it happens so often that it may be considered a general rule." Also L. F. Alfred Maury, in 1877,* said that anxiety or desire, though during the day not at all pronounced, acquired in sleep the strength of confirmed suspicions; and that our innate instincts and impulses, sleep overmastering reflection and considerations of policy, were set free to have all their own way.

By " innate instincts and impulses," Maury, of course, meant what Freud calls the unconscious; it is the source of our energy, and of the feeling that life is worth living. It is certainly revealed in action in our dreams; is it revealed in a perceptible form, in any other way? The answer is, In a disguised form, as in dreams, Yes.

Slips of the pen and of the tongue are a common form; so are impulsive gestures and characteristic tones of voice. People judge these things instinctively, that is, by the exercise of their unconscious; in other words, unconscious calls to unconscious. Anger is betrayed by a tone in the voice, not only to men, but to animals; the dog can understand his master's words without understanding

* " La Magie et L'Astrologie."

his master's vocabulary. The host may say kind words to his guest, but, if he does not really mean them (*i.e.*, if they are conscious, arisen from a sense of duty or obligation, and not the true unconscious wishes) the guest will instinctively realize that they are false. Or if one receives a letter like this: " I shall be very pleased to meet you tonight at the concert," one knows, or ought to, that the word crossed out conveys the unconscious and real meaning of the writer, and the substituted word only a forced and false meaning. Again, if one instinctively avoids the gaze of some one else, the cause is either, strong love or strong hatred (as La Bruyère partly remarked in his " Characters "). Prince Hamlet's " play within a play " was designed to force an unconscious confession from King Claudius, who, seeing acted before him the very crime he had himself committed, betrayed his guilt by turning pale, groaning aloud, and rushing from the chamber, calling

"Give me some light; — away!"

Such behavior speaks louder than words.

Thus, in Freud's view,* our little unintentional actions are not casual or accidental at all, for they are weighted by the unconscious, and betray our inmost thoughts and desires, what we least

* " The Psychopathology of Everyday Life."

wish to expose, and what we least suppose we are exposing. " Mr. Y. falls in love with a lady who soon thereafter marries Mr. X. In spite of the fact that Mr. Y. was an old acquaintance of Mr. X.'s, and had business relations with him, he repeatedly forgot the name, and on a number of occasions, when wishing to correspond with X. he was obliged to ask other people for his name. Here the motivation for forgetting is obvious, and it is a direct result of Y.'s dislike for his successful rival, he wishes to blot him out."

A patient will tell his doctor that he is afraid to cross open spaces, and believes that that is the whole of the matter; but it is not the whole explanation, it is only the part he is consciously aware of — there is something left unsaid, because it lies shrouded in the unconscious. The doctor can cure the man, if he finds out, by dreams or other indirect means, what the hidden thought is; and that is why the study of dreams is so important for the treatment of nervous disease.

As the unconscious wields so great a power over the personality, it is of interest to know what dreams are common to great numbers of people; and, in this connection, a good deal has been done, as, for instance, in the record and classification of the dreams of London school children,* which

* See " Address to the Child Study Society," by Dr. C. W. Kimmins, Chief Inspector to the London Education Committee, as reported in the " Times Educational Supplement," February 20, 1919.

has been undertaken by Dr. C. W. Kimmins. Children under five related their dreams to headmistresses; older children described them in writing receiving instructions to " write a full and true account of the last dream you can remember; state your age, and also say about how long ago you had the dream you have described." The answers totalled five thousand.

Like primitive man, very young cannot distinguish dream action from real life; nor can they express their dreams clearly in words. The difficulty is increased by the tendency to fill up gaps by improvised material from their fancy, and to reject incidents that run contrary to experience.

Reliable detailed analysis is thus put out of the question; but information of a general kind can be gathered from the records, which divide the dreams up into groups under such headings as, wishes, fears, air-raids, fairy stories, domestic, burglars, and the like.

Twenty-five per cent of the dreams of very young children come under this heading of fear. The dreams are generally of wicked men, and when the record was made these were mostly Germans. At five years old the child always occupies the chief place in the story, his individuality now developing. This is one dream of a boy of that age: " I dreamed that a tiger came into our house and ate mummy and daddy and my brother and me, and then I woke up and cried and said, ' It isn't true ' '"; and this is one of a girl, the night after the King and Queen had paid a visit to Peckham — " A lady was sitting on my bed, and the King and Queen were under the bed eating bread and butter, and a lot of ladies with them." At this stage, dreaming and waking elements are still mixed at seven, the dream becomes detached, as a thing apart from real experience), and family relationships are not understood.

In the years from five to seven, Christmas and Santa Claus frequently appear; and at seven, both boys and girls have more burglar dreams than at any other age, and boys (girls are never much affected by it) many cinema dreams. Boys at this age show a bias towards hunting wild animals, and girls towards fairies and domestic life. The fairy tales have a happy ending, except now and then when a witch pops in. Ghost stories are rare, and so are scenes of school activities, whether work or play.

Logical sequence is generally conspicuous by its absence. Consider this example: A girl who is swimming to save a friend from drowning meets a teacher in the water, who orders her to return at once to school because she has been chosen to take the part of Julius Caesar in the play. Or this: A girl's father and mother are transformed into cabbages, and she prepares them for dinner. They turn back into her father and mother, and ask her how she likes aeroplanes.

Dr. Kimmins* comes to the following conclusions: Children's dreams differ from adults in several ways; they are in closer relation to the child's temperament, they overflow more freely from the previous day (*e.g.*, many of the dreams satisfy the desires forbidden fulfilment by parents and teachers), they are more colored by secondary elaboration, and finally, they tend, far more than adults' to correspond literally with the desires they express.

The very common dream of falling, gliding, or floating in air or water (the kinæsthetic dream) is rare in children under nine years old, but then increases steadily, most of all in well fed children, up to the age of eighteen.

Records and deductions of this sort, when derived from large bodies of people, help to show what is at the basis of their thoughts; it is a sort of gigantic confessional, and the psychologist is a father-confessor who can alleviate some of the distress of the world, by advocating that treatment of mankind that its real, and not its apparent nature, needs.

* " Children's Dreams," by C. W. Kimmins, M.A., D.Sc.

The psycho-analysis of one and three-quarter millions of American recruits showed that out of every forty there was one of less mental development than that of a normal child of ten.

CHAPTER VIII

DREAM ANALYSIS: FREUD

" Dream analysis is the *via regia* to the Unconscious." — *Freud.*

" What we wish to recognize is, that apparently a terrible species of wild and lawless appetites resides in every one of us, even when in some cases we have the appearance of being perfectly self-restrained. And this fact, it seems, becomes evident in sleep." — *Plato*, Book IX of " The Republic."

IN the last chapter an attempt was made to indicate in what manner desires lurking in the unconscious work themselves out in dreams; but the practical utility of the Freudian theory lies rather in the reverse process of finding out from given dreams what the generating unconscious desires were. When the patient knows what are his prevailing unconscious desires, he can check their undermining influence by consciously combating them; for instance, if A is unconsciously wishing to see his father, who is dead, he can prevent a nervous breakdown, once he knows the wish is there, by firmly declaring that he does *not* want to see him. The physician's problem, therefore, in treating a nervous case, is to discover, by dreams or some other means, what is the patient's unconscious wish; and the process of doing this is called psycho-analysis.

Of course, when the dream is a direct wish fulfilment there is no difficulty at all. Freud described the case of a medical student whose besetting sin was unpunctuality. One morning, when the maid called him as usual, saying " get up; you have to go to the hospital," he only half awoke, and immediately dreamed of a ward in the hospital, where he lay on a bed, with the regulation card of particulars hung up on the wall above his head. Muttering, " Since I'm already in the hospital, I don't need to get up and go there," he turned over on his side, and went on sleeping comfortably.

But it is rare that dreams are facilely direct, like this one. They require careful analysis.

One day in 1897, Freud heard — and he was delighted at the news — that two of the professors of his university (Vienna) had proposed him for the vacant post of " professor extraordinarius." A colleague, who had been waiting some time to hear whether *his* nomination to a similar chair had been a success, coming in to see Freud, told him that he had consulted a high authority, who expressed a fear that his religion and nationality would stand in his way. As it happened that Freud was of the same religion and nationality he at once began to take a gloomy view of his prospects.

" On the morning after this visit," writes Freud, " I had the following dream."

I. Friend R is my uncle. I feel tender affection for him.

II. I see his face somewhat altered before me. It is, as it were, drawn out lengthwise, a yellow beard that surrounds it stands out with exceptional clearness."

At first he dismissed the dream as an absurdity; but when he remembered that if his patients had dreams like this it portended painful wishes, such as they would not willingly avow, he at once set to work on its analysis in detail, noting down, while so doing, all the ideas that entered his mind.

He recognized that the face in the dream was composite, consisting partly of the face of his friend R (who had talked over the prospects of a chair with him), and partly that of one of his uncles, who had recently been on his trial at the courts of justice. Freud's father had been in the habit of saying that the uncle's downfall had been due to weakmindedness rather than to wickedness; and so, by association, the dream expressed the fact that the friend R was similarly weak-minded.

Then he recognized the source of the long-drawn face: it belonged to another colleague, who had also been nominated without success for a chair, and who had stated, in conversation, that he attributed it to an accusation brought against him by one of his patients, which was none the less fatal to his cause though the charge had been dismissed by the courts as unfounded and malicious.

Reconstructing the dream, Freud concludes that the uncle's face composite with that of one colleague and altering into that of another, both of whom had failed to get professorships, meant that he thought one was stupid and the other criminal, and that their non-success was due to these facts, and not to their nationality or religion.

This assumption of the unconscious — this fulfilled wish — would reanimate Freud's hopes, and dissipate his forebodings; but naturally so mean a wish would be intolerable to Freud's conscious thoughts, it would be repressed to the unconscious, which, in its turn, gave vent to its spleen in a disguised form in the dream. The tender affection felt in the dream being much stronger than his real regard for either uncle or friends, was no part of the unconscious wish, but rather contrary to it; it was produced by the displacement of the intense hatred of his colleagues by the small liking for his uncle, as a means of disguise to evade the censor.

It will thus be seen that to psycho-analyze a dream, the first thing to do is to recall the dream to mind in every detail, and to make a note of the several particulars of it, — each person, object, scene, word, feeling, action. The next thing to do is to consider each of these particulars by itself, try to identify it from your experience, and to recollect everything else associated with it in your memory. The principal wish at the basis of the dream can then be sifted out, — many particulars converging on one point — and the meaning of the dream will be clear.

A hysterical patient of Freud's dreamed repeatedly that there was a smell of a pudding burning. At first she persisted in denying ever having known such a smell attracting her attention; but finally it was brought to her mind that at the crisis of her unhappy love-affair she had been employed in baking a pudding, which had been overdone. In her conscious mind, she had forgotten the incident; and so it was all the more suited to act as a symbol for her repressed love to use in order to evade the censor and obtain imaginary fulfilment.

One day a certain lady consulting a physician in Harley Street cried, " Doctor, I am an absolute wreck. I used to be *so* happy and careless, and now I am nothing like myself, but nervous and depressed. Oh! what can I do, Doctor? "

" Have you anything painful on your mind? " he inquired.

" No, nothing to speak of," she answered.

" Perhaps you dream a good deal? "

" Yes, I do," she replied, hysterically, " Why, in this last week, I have had the same dream thrice."

" I see. Good. Would you mind telling me what it was? "

" Oh! " she replied, " it is too absurd for words. It wouldn't interest you in the slightest."

" That's quite all right," he replied, " but I am very anxious to hear it all the same; so *would* you kindly describe it."

" Well," she answered at last, " it was simply this. There was a round table, and a little white terrier with a black spot on its nose, was racing round and round it. Then I woke up. Quite absurd, as you see."

" Thank you," said the doctor, making a note of the particulars. " Now, tell me, do you recollect seeing a table like that at any time? "

" No, I don't think so."

" But consider the matter carefully. Have you such a table in your home? "

" No, we haven't. But now I come to think of it, one of my friends has."

" Good. Now, what about the little white dog?"

" I think that is easily explained. It belongs to the same friend; and she came to see me only last Monday."

" Has *it* a black spot on its nose? "

" No. But there was a photograph on Monday in the ' Daily — ' of a mascot spotted like that, and my friend and I laughed, saying how funny

Toby, her dog, would look, with a black spot on his nose."

" Thank you. Now, please tell me about your friend's visit last Monday."

" Oh! she came, as she often does, for afternoon tea, bringing Toby with her. We just talked about the usual things, till about five, when Toby began barking and jumping up at the table. My husband was the cause; he was coming up the stairs, and the dog had heard him; and as for me, my heart sank, because, I'm sorry to say, I loathe my husband."

" Loathe him? "

" Yes, absolutely. At one time we were fairly happy, but gradually we drifted apart, we had little in common, and I grew to loathe him, and long to get a divorce. However, to keep my mind from dwelling on it, I plunged into a whirl of social life, and helped in charity organization; and now I have broken down altogether."

" Madam," said the physician, " your dreams make it quite clear what your nerves are due to: it is this, you are worrying about the divorce. The heavy work you have been doing has lowered your power of resistance, until now you can recover only by one of two means: you must decide, once for all, whether you *do* want this divorce or whether you don't, if the latter you must break down the barrier between your husband

and you, and if the former, you must take steps at once to obtain a divorce. So will you please think the matter carefully over for a week, make up your mind on the question finally, and then come back here and inform me of your decision."

"Certainly," she answered, "I will. Thank you ever so much."

A week later, the lady returned, looking bright and cheerful, and saw the physician again.

"Well," said he cordially, "have you made up up your mind? Why, you look well again already."

"Yes, I feel well, too," she answered smiling. "My story is very short; for, when I faced the question out, and considered so drastic a step as divorce, I somehow felt differently towards my husband. I went to him frankly; there were mutual explanations; and now, I assure you, I don't even think of a divorce."

"Excellent," said the physician; "rest a few weeks from your work, go to the seaside for a change of air, and you will be quite strong again. Good-day."

And she was gone, her trouble removed.

But why should the physician's questions almost infallibly lead the patient to reveal the complex which is at the root of his trouble? The patient thinks that he is giving free associations, *i.e.*, ideas unconnected with a pre-existing scheme; but he is not. As was explained of slips of the tongue and of the pen, his ideas are controlled by "unconscious trends of activity," and so the thoughts that arise are prompted and selected in relation to the central complex; it therefore follows, that when the associations are tracked down from each separate component of the patient's dream, they all converge on one point, namely, the desire that originally generated the dream, and so, if the patient is neurotic, the complex causing the breakdown.

As soon as this complex is known, it again comes under the control of the foreconscious, and so a firm denial in the conscious will undo the repression. The best proof of this lies in the success of treatment given on those lines in innumerable nervous cases; the patients do recollect the origin of their trouble, corroboration is forthcoming from other sources, and cures are regular. Moreover masses of people react like individuals to natural laws; and Dr. Rivers has shown* that the customs and beliefs of savages evolve, like dreams, through process of condensation, displacement, symbolic dramatization, and secondary elaboration, and serve the end of outlets for suppressed wishes. " Even so disputable a part of Freud's scheme," he adds, " as his doctrine of the ' censor ' has its definite counterpart in savage culture."

As for corroborative evidence of the true

* " Dreams and Primitive Culture," 1917–1918.

nature of a patient's complex, Dr. Jung's test of waking associations is final. The procedure is as follows. The physician has a list of words, which suggest most of the common needs and interests of life; and this he reads out very slowly, word by word, after instructing the patient to think of each word as he hears it, and then reply as quickly as he can with the very first word that enters his mind. The replies are written down, and also the intervals that elapse (in fifths of a second) between the repetition of the stimulus word and the occurrence of the reply word. This is done on the principle that, whenever a word read by the physician awakens a memory connected with the suppressed desire, the patient will answer in a different way, and take a different time to react to the stimulus, from when the ideas awakened are such as he is indifferent to. Here is the list.

JUNG'S ASSOCIATION TEST *

1 head	10 friendly	19 pride
2 green	11 to cook	20 table
3 water	12 to ask	21 ink
4 to sing	13 cold	22 angry
5 dead	14 stem	23 needle
6 long	15 to dance	24 to swim
7 ship	16 village	25 voyage
8 to pay	17 lake	26 blue
9 window	18 sick	27 lamp

* See " Collected Papers on Analytical Psychology," by C. G. Jung, M.D., LL.D. (Ballière, Tindall & Cox, 1916).

28 to sin	53 hunger	77 cow
29 bread	54 white	78 friend
30 rich	55 child	79 luck
31 tree	56 to take care	80 lie
32 to prick	57 lead pencil	81 deportment
33 pity	58 sad	82 narrow
34 yellow	59 plum	83 brother
35 mountain	60 to marry	84 to fear
36 to die	61 house	85 stork
37 salt	62 dear	86 false
38 new	63 glass	87 anxiety
39 custom	64 to quarrel	88 to kiss
40 to pray	65 fur	89 bride
41 money	66 big	90 pure
42 foolish	67 carrot	91 door
43 pamphlet	68 to paint	92 to choose
44 despise	69 part	93 hay
45 finger	70 old	94 contented
46 expensive	71 flower	95 ridicule
47 bird	72 to beat	96 to sleep
48 to fall	73 box	97 mouth
49 book	74 wild	98 nice
50 unjust	75 family	99 woman
51 frog	76 to wash	100 to abuse
52 to part		

Of course, the replies are usually meaningless in themselves, and appear to the patient useless and absurd; but they indirectly reveal any unconscious trends. The answers, might be head-tail; green-blue; water-wine; to sing-song; dead-alive; long-short; ship-boat; to pay-money. But these are not the important thing, which is rather whether the time taken is long or short (the average normal time is 1–1/5 seconds), and whether the same answer occurs twice or more.

Suppose that A took five seconds to reply to A 1. (Money), then one would suspect some worry under that head; and if the answer were " bag," and the same answer were made to numbers 61 (house), 84 (to fear), and 8 (to pay), one would feel confirmed in the suspicion, and led to think that the money was either for a house, or with a house as surety. Cross-examination would help to expose the facts.

To all of numbers 88 (to kiss), 89 (bride), 90 (pure), 92 (to choose), 93 (hay), 94 (contented), 98 (nice), 99 (woman), a certain subject replied, " pink ": he was engaged to a girl who had worn a pink costume when he last saw her, and he ardently desired to be able to marry her soon — while a poor salary checked his hopes.

A young barrister of extraordinary talents and brilliant promise, with every confidence in himself, suddenly changed in demeanor, becoming nervous in manner, shrinking from encountering people — he began to go to the courts in a closed cab through unfrequented streets — and finally became changed into a hysterical wreck, too apprehensive even to leave his own bedroom. At this stage, a specialist was called in.

First, the patient was questioned about his dreams, but without results; then Jung's Association Test was tried. In his answers there were obvious peculiarities both in time of reaction,

and in frequent repetitions. Numbers 1 (head),
4 (to sing), 12 (to ask), 33 (to pity), 36 (to die),
40 (to pray), 52 (to part), 62 (dear), 75 (family),
88 (to kiss), all received answer " Mother," and
all had reaction times of over two seconds.

" Have you any worries? " asked the physician.

" No," replied the young barrister.

" How is your mother, may I ask? "

" Oh, she is dead," was the eager answer.
" She died a long while ago, but I often think of
her still."

" Would you mind telling me about her? "

" Not at all. You see, as a little child I was
very nervous and delicate, and so mother made
a great fuss of me. The children I used to play
with were often rough, and then I used to run
away from them, and find a refuge in my mother's
arms. But she died when I was only six. The
awful difference it made to me I leave you to
imagine. Whenever I was buffeted about, I still
wanted to run to mother, but she was there no
more. And I have cherished her memory very
dearly."

" Thank you. Then let me explain what you
are worrying about; it is exactly what you have
just narrated — you are longing still to be literally
in your mother's arms."

" Surely not; why, it doesn't sound possible,"
replied the patient.

" That may be, but it is true none the less. When your mother died, you evidently repressed, not consciously — for you were unwilling to realize her death — your wish to run to her arms; but the heavy work of the last year having reduced your powers of resistance, the long-repressed desire gained the upper hand, and played havoc with your nerves. You must conquer that wish consciously, and this time kill the snake, not scotch it. Now, *do* you want to be in your mother's arms? "

" Of course I don't, it's impossible and absurd."

" Good. Then go away to the seaside for three months' change of air and rest, and keep telling yourself, like a prayer, that you don't want to be in the arms of your mother: and you will soon be as strong and sound as ever you were. Goodday."

And three months after, surely enough, the rising young barrister was at the courts again, and as successful as he had been before.

One has but to try Jung's Word Test on one's friends to find out how it works; and no doubt unexpected revelations will be obtained from quite normal people. It will be found also, that certain types of answers occur over and over again; and simple laws have been established depending on this observation.

The instruction given is that a single word is

the response required; if, therefore, the subject gives several words instead, it betrays a neurotic character, tending to offer others more feeling than the occasion requires — he adds explanatory statements to his answer. Freud calls this a " reinforced object-libido," which means that compensation is made, by pouring out energy pell-mell, for an inner want of contentment or stabilized feelings. People afflicted with it are painfully nervous, and easily carried away.

Answers by contrast are common, *e.g.*, big-little, white-black, old-young; but they do not indicate any special tendency; on the other hand, descriptions like flower-pretty, knife-dangerous, sing-heavenly, reveal by their excess of feeling an inner want of feeling, a normal answer being rather, *e.g.*, flower-bud, knife-fork, sing-dance, which are objective and unemotional. These emotional answers are rare with children, but common with women over forty, and men over sixty.

The normal subject's answers are objective, and are uttered after a short and regular interval the normal stupid or affectedly clever subjects are equal in time of response, but consist mostly of definitions, *e.g.*, Table — a piece of household furniture; the neurotic's, being disturbed by a complex, are very irregular in time of response, and are obviously emotionalized.

To make the deductions accurate, the data may be checked in several ways. The list of words is repeated, and the subject is asked to give the same answer as before, to the best of his ability. In normal cases false reproductions are fewer than twenty per cent; in neurotic cases, often as many as forty per cent. The neurotic's complex (*i.e.*, system of repressed wishes) forms an obstacle to the memory; and so the false reproductions give a further indication of the source of the patient's trouble, and their percentage is a rough gauge of his emotivity.

A complex may be suspected should any of the following irregularities be observed: a prolonged reaction time; no answer vouchsafed; more than one word given (*e.g.*, supplementary illustrations); a repetition of the stimulus word; the same answer to different stimulus words; a superficial association especially with long reaction time; a meaningless reaction; the stimulus word is mis-read, misunderstood, or taken in an unusual sense; or when there is a high percentage of incorrect reproductions.

Suppose the patient's complex discovered; how did it arise, and how can it be cured?

The unconscious, " a wild beast caged in the heart of a city,"* is the source of our temptations and sins; it prompts selfish thoughts and sensual

* Freud.

desires. However, we can resist them. If we do so, and recognize the temptations frankly *as* temptations, our highly organized conscious will support our resistance with a powerful force of moral and social wishes, by the aid of which we may defeat the unconscious desire. This last is not utterly destroyed, once and for all, however, by this resistance, but may gather his forces together to deliver a second attack, and a third, each ending in a pitched battle. But the danger is worse when the temptation is not frankly faced — namely, when one shrinks from it with disgust. So when a gently-nurtured and conventional girl, dimly apprehending temptation, is too horrified to consider it frankly in the full light of day, and pushes the thoughts out of her mind almost before they have arisen, she is not defended by the full power of her moral sense, and the repressed thoughts seethe in secret in the subterranean passages of the mind, and gather to a head for a more determined onslaught when the conscious is next off its guard. During the day, the censor is too watchful; but by night, while he dozes, the repressed desires obtain satisfaction in a subtly camouflaged symbolic dream.

A time may come when, from overwork or chronic fatigue the censor is disabled for action; and then the lurking enemy wreaks its revenge unchecked, takes full possession of the girl's conscious, and brings about what, for want of a better term, is called a "nervous breakdown." The conscious has become helpless, having never truly realized the enemy-temptation, and having no weapons with which to fight an unseen foe.

But can relief be obtained, or is it too late? It is not too late if the girl learns what the temptation is, and faces it clearly in thought, however repulsive it may be; for then the conscious can still summon up its reserves, and fight the open enemy — a pitched battle ensues on a clear issue, and with perseverance, the conscious, or moral and social party, will win a decisive victory. The "nervous breakdown" will then soon cease. And that is why it is essential to trace out the exact form of the complex (*i.e.*, temptation, worry or fear); and why it is of the utmost importance in nervous cases to examine the patient's dreams.

The justification and proof of the essential truth of psycho-analysis rests thus in its fruits, namely, the undoubted alleviation of the sufferings of thousands of nerve patients. At the same time, as with Darwin's theories in the last century, a great deal of opposition has been made both to the theory as a whole, and still more to the details and extreme generalizations. Many objections come from the conservative type of psychologist who objects to the theory just because it is new; others come from religious and moral teachers who are alarmed at the prospect of a clash with some of their predilections; but still a substantial body of criticism is left, from open-minded thinkers with no special prejudices.

Of the grossly prejudiced type of criticism, there is the example of Dr. Frederick van Eeden.* He, while admitting that some dreams are explicable by Freud's theory, claims that a large number cannot be so explained, as they are brought to us by demons in the night, who inveigle them into our brains, with a maleficent purpose!

Of the saner sort, Dr. William McDougall,† admitting many of Freud's contentions, repudiates the conclusions of Freud's more enthusiastic followers, especially in their assertion that all dreams arise from repressed tendencies. It may be replied to this that Jung's investigations, using the word test, point just as surely to repressed tendencies as the source of nervous disturbance, and very often confirm the very complexes already discovered by a study of the patients' dreams.

Another open-minded authority, Brevet Lieutenant-Colonel F. W. Mott, M.D., F.R.S.,‡ etc., also allows that Freud is right in his main contention, but argues that the sexual motive, which Freud considers the be-all and end-all of the unconscious, is by no means the only one,

* " Proceedings of the S. P. R., Vol. XXVI, 1912–13, p. 43 *et seq.*
† " Psychology, the Study of Behaviour."
‡ *The Lancet*, Vol. I, 1918, p. 169. '

another being, for example, the desire for self-preservation. Dreams, he urges, arise from the two fundamental motives for action, self-conservation and the propagation of the species. Dr. Morton Prince would add still other motives, such as doubt, scruples, and worries; but it is surely obvious that these are only negative wishes and nervous conflicts, such as are already fully comprehended in Freud's system.

Further light is thrown on the broad question of the Freudian principles by the ethnological studies of Dr. W. H. R. Rivers, M.A.,M.D., F.R.S.* "According to Freud," he says, " every dream expresses the fulfilment of a wish, the most prominent underlying motive of every dream being some wish on the part of the dreamer. That a vast number of dreams can be so explained stands beyond all doubt, the expression being sometimes direct and subject to no special transformation, especially in the case of children and uneducated persons. There are, however, many dreams which can only be explained on these lines if the term ' wish ' be used in an indirect and unusual sense, whereas they receive a natural explanation if they be the expression of some other emotional state such as anxiety, fear or shame. Desire is only one, though probably the

* " Dreams and Primitive Culture," a lecture at the Rylands Library, Manchester, April 10, 1918.

most frequent, of the affective states to which dreams are due." This is no stinted corroboration. "According to Freud," he continues, "sexual motives form the prominent elements in the experience which is manifested in the dream. Freud uses the term 'sexual' with a far wider connotation than that usually assigned to it in common speech, but even if this be taken into account, there is no doubt that he has over-rated the frequency with which sexual elements enter into the production of the dream, while many of his disciples have far outrun in this respect the discretion of their master. Freud himself has provided us with abundant evidence in his ' Traum-deutung ' that dreams may depend on such motives as professional jealousy, self-reproaches concerning patients, and other affective states incident upon the life and work of a physician." But here Dr. Rivers forgets that these last are only the occasion of dreams, while the energy derived by them from the unconscious to render them powerful enough for the purpose of the dream work may well be sexual all the same.

Dr. Rivers goes on to examine our knowledge of the rites and customs of primitive peoples, and he comes to the conclusion that they symbolize racial wishes and fears, exactly as dreams symbolize the individual's wishes and fears; furthermore, he finds in the process of formation of primitive rites and customs stages precisely analogous to those of the dream work, namely, condensation, displacement, dramatization, and finally secondary elaboration. "It is not necessary here," he asserts, "to dwell on the opposition that these views (*i.e.*, Freud's theories) have aroused, except to say that they form the best possible witness to their originality and to the justness of Freud's discovery if the future should prove him to be right. The fact that resemblances so close should have been found in another aspect of human thought and action might well be held to provide striking confirmation of the truth of Freud's interpretation of dreams."

Later, he adds, "It is an essential part, if not the most essential part, of Freud's scheme that the dream reveals the unconscious, that the thoughts which are manifested in the dream as we immediately experience it do not enter into consciousness in ordinary waking states. . . . The more deeply one goes on in dream analysis, the more certain does it become that dreams are essentially expressions of the unconscious. Even in those cases in which the manifest content of a dream seems at first sight to be wholly explained by recent occurrences, further study shows the existence of deeper meanings and general trends of mentation belonging to levels which do not ordinarily enter into manifest consciousness. . . . Any one who has attempted to discover explanations of rude rites and customs from those who practice them will have no hesitation in accepting their origin in the unconscious."

Finally, he concludes, " The object of this lecture has been to make out a preliminary case for the essential similarity of two manifestations of the early stages of mental development; the dream as the expression of the infantile mentality of the individual; savage rite and custom as the expression of the primitive or infantile mentality of the race."

And so *The Lancet*, in a leading article (February 23, 1918, p. 298) said, " There can be no doubt, if we are to judge by analogous historical instances in the realm of thought, that what in the doctrine of Freud is not shaken by criticism will remain and fructify."

And we may leave it safely at that.

CHAPTER IX

DREAM ANALYSIS: JUNG

" Be ye well-advised to be afeared of a dream-reader? " said King Lot.
— *Malory.*

" The dream for me is, in the first instance, the subliminal picture
of the psychological condition of the individual in his waking state."
— *Jung,* " Collected Papers on Analytical Psychology."

CONSIDER this dream. " I am walking from my
place of residence to the   Tube Station, carrying
two top hats, and trying rather vainly, burdened
as I am, to hold an umbrella up, I arrive at the
station later than usual; and, the umbrella having been no protection from the rain, I am wet
through."

What is the meaning of this?

By Freud's method, we should take each fea-
ture of the story in turn, trace it back to the life
experience of the dreamer, and inquire into the
wishes connected with it.

Let us then question the dreamer.

Dreamer. You ask me about an umbrella.
Yes, I carry one regularly.

Freudian. Have you had any trouble lately,
connected with one?

Dreamer. Oh yes, just yesterday, in fact. Through business worries, I had slept badly and got up late; and, to crown all, I forgot to take my umbrella with me. As luck would have it, it was raining hard, and I got soaked through.

Freudian. Good. Now when have you lately paid special regard to a top hat, or made remarks about them, or disliked some one wearing one?

Dreamer. I can't recollect anything important. However, last Sunday at church, when I was wearing a bowler myself, I saw two old friends who were wearing top hats, and I envied them their prosperity, while at the same time inwardly hoping that my present business ventures, in spite of a bad start, might succeed in the end, and raise me to a position like theirs.

Freudian. And what does the Tube Station mean to you in life, something pleasant or unpleasant?

Dreamer. Well, every morning as I enter the station, I think of the days soon to come, I hope, when I shall be well enough off to have no further need to make this daily business journey. And yet, on the other hand, I dread the possible ill-success that threatens to defeat all my hopes. But, by the way, just last Sunday, in church, the top hats I saw made me think how shabbily my wife and I have to dress; and I hoped to be able very soon to afford better things.

Freudian. Good. Now, I think, the meaning of your dream is quite clear, it is the fulfilment of your wish for success in business, escape from an impending calamity, easier circumstances for yourself and your wife, and deliverance from your petty daily restrictions.

It is noticeable, in this exposition, that though it may explain the *cause* of the dream, it has little bearing on the future, and serves in no sense to help the dreamer to solve his difficulties — except insofar as it forces upon him a clearer realization of his position.

Jung goes a step farther than this: he gives the dream a meaning, from which the dreamer can learn what policy he should pursue in the future. Jung leaves the question of the cause out of account, and instead feels forward towards a solution. He admits the· Freudian interpretation, but insists that there is a symbolic meaning too, of great import, and much wider application. Thus, a Jungian physician might treat the top hat dream in the following way.

Jungian. Your two top hats stand for two unadjusted sides to your life, or two obstacles that lie in your way — perhaps your business and your home life, or money affairs and public support for your new venture; and thus the lesson of the dream is this, that you should at once proceed to regulate these two sides of your life, and try to overcome the obstacles in your path. Meanwhile the dream has helped to keep you cheerful, by compensating you in your imagination.

Dr. Maurice Nicoll* describes the case of a girl of seventeen, who reported her dream thus: " I was walking down the street where our house is when suddenly some soldiers wearing helmets came round a corner. They stopped me, and one of them grasped my arm. I woke in terror."

This would be a wish fulfilment, on Freud's system, thinly disguised, and ultimately traceable back to a sexual desire: the girl probably desired to evade a calamity impending from the war, the nature of the calamity being traceable by cross examining her about each detail of the story. It would be in a different way that Jung would treat the dream; he would look *forward*. The girl had been stimulated by the advent of the war, which had opened up fresh avenues of excitement for her: she was afraid of war risks, as the dream at first suggests, but of something more general, namely, dangers, or menacing factors, in her own life development. The war was a national menace as sex was an individual menace; and the dream signifies that the girl, who was on the threshold of womanhood, was about to confront the unrealized menace of sex; and the dream might be looked upon as a foreshadowing of her transition from

* " Dream Psychology," by Maurice Nicoll, B.A., M.B., B.C. (Camb.)

girl to woman. The lesson taught by it is: realize the change that is taking place, and be very cautious in the new rôle.

Dr. Nicoll reported another soldier dream, of a married woman who maintained that she cared nothing about the war, her interests being concerned with other things; and her dream was as follows: " I heard a noise and got up to look out of the window. I saw soldiers in the garden. The moonlight shone on their helmets. They were all round the house. I tried to call out for my husband, but he was fast asleep, and I was so helpless with terror that I could not make any sound."

This would be interpreted by Freud as fulfilment in imagination of her desire that they would not (or fear that they would) take her husband away from her to serve in the army. By Jung, it would be interpreted creatively, as a purposeful activity in her nervous economy. The dreamer's pretended indifference to the war was a mere pose; ignoring duty and patriotism, she clung fondly to the hope of her husband's permanent exemption from service. As a result, to compensate for her one-sided ideas during the day, her mind turned at night to the opposite extreme of thought: her husband is lying asleep, and she cannot call him, while her thoughts are devoted to the war idea. She flees from the menaces of the time by day, but by night they haunt her sleep.

The lesson is: face the fact bravely that the husband may have to go, and don't shirk your duty.

Thus, in Jung's view of dreams, compensation for one-sidedness is a common function, to set up a balance of the outlets of our wishes; a " breakdown " consisting of extreme one-sidedness. It is a matter of frequent observation. Arctic explorers, when their food rations run short, will have pleasant dreams of the most delicious tarts and pastries, representative of just the delicacies that they cannot possibly hope for. A poor peasant girl will have dreams of a handsome prince, who is to take her away with him, and make her his wife in a handsome castle. There is then, as it were, an agency working in our minds to repair the manifest inequalities of our fortune by implanting hopes of better days.

"Hope springs eternal in the human breast;
Man never is, but always to be blest."

Hope enables us the better to grapple with our difficulties, and find contentment amidst poverty. Jung calls the agency our fantasy-building system. This it is which, in our dreams, gives us the satisfaction denied to our waking eyes; and this it is also that induces people to boast of their income, ability and prowess; it is thus a protection from the temptation to despair, and a safeguard of our happiness.

Which, then, is the more useful view to take,

Freud's or Jung's? Should some one, asleep in a swamp, with a storm raging overhead, and jackals howling around, dream of pleasant days at home with wife and family; would we be wiser to interpret this with Freud as a wish fulfilment, or with Jung as compensation for the painful straits he is in?

Jung's followers, and Dr. Maurice Nicoll among them, accuse the former of narrowness, as it leads back merely to the central motive of sexual love; they claim that the primary purpose of dreams is to alleviate the unpleasant conditions and limitations of life, by making an adjustment during sleep, and so to preserve the balance of sanity — wish fulfilment answering a secondary purpose only. But as both views serve a very useful end, Freud's to cure the ill results of the past, and Jung's to prevent ill results in the future, there is little need to take sides violently in the dispute. The two schools are not antagonistic the one to the other, but they are rather complementary.

Jung's view helps to account for the excess of fantasy in children. They are not ripe yet to face the world, and its disillusioning experiences, so nature has given them the protection of a sort of woolly envelope to deaden the shocks of reality; but as children develop, they may gradually discard this protection. The more sensitive the child is, the more he needs the protection of compensating fantasies; and we say of him that it would be bad for him to be too soon disillusioned. This is a more satisfying explanation than Freud's, who would call the dreams a mere wish fulfilment.

The same protection is afforded by the fantasy-building system to adults who dread the shock of disastrous news. Thus, during the war, a woman whose husband was reported missing firmly rejected the idea that he was dead, and invented a plausible story of her own to account for the official report. By this means, she preserved her sanity, and went on with her work sufficiently happily; and so, as she was thus enabled to perform a useful task in the community, the fantasy was not only a private safeguard but a public benefit.

Lesser fantasies serve ends as useful. The fantasy of a peasant girl dreaming of marriage with a prince impels her to improve herself in order to be worthy of a prince; the English predilection for the ideal of a " gentleman," is symbolic and compensatory, and supplies an ideal for ordinary folk to live by; the same function is performed in America by the idea of a millionaire, and in France by the idea of woman; so in pre-war Germany, the fantasy ideal was the Kaiser.

However, compensation can easily run to an extreme, and prove worse than none at all.

Fantasies may take a ludicrous form, claim a fanatical belief, and render the person lunatic; whereas had there been no compensation at all, he would merely have been a morbid pessimist. It is moderate fantasy-building that is the mainstay of sanity; and so nothing is more cruel than to tamper rudely with any one's favorite beliefs, however ridiculous and false they seem to us; this is to form a stumbling-block to his soul's content — it were indeed better that a millstone were hanged about our neck, and that we were cast into the sea. National prejudices (*i.e.*, fantasies) serve the end of galvanizing a people, so that they may work harmoniously towards a common end; and likewise rumor in time of war affords compensation for bad news, or for sudden success, and so stimulates the nation to yet greater efforts.

In common with so many other medical authorities, Jung will not limit the motive-power of dreams to sexual desire alone; he admits, as coordinate motives, anger, fear, hunger, thirst, fatigue, jealousy and self-preservation. It is probable, however, that ultimately the difference will be found to consist more in terminology than in fact.

Further, he extends the meaning of the manifest content. Freud presents it as the dramatization, on principles of association, of the individual wishes of the psyche. Jung regards it as a kind of barometer reading of the person's nervous state; in his own words,* " it presents a résumé of the subliminal associative material which is brought together by the momentary psychological situation."

A dream is thus at once a species of imaginative compensation for real one-sidedness of life, and a symbolic diagnosis of our case and its solution. " To the Zürich school," Jung remarks, " the symbol is not merely a sign of something repressed and concealed, but is at the same time an attempt to comprehend and to point out the way of the further psychological development of the individual."

The advantage of this conception over Freud's lies in its philosophy; the mind can keep its wings free for daring future flights, whatever the past may have been, whereas, with Freud's conception, the mind has its wings of hope chipped by an iron shears of predestination. As we look backward from the dream to the sexual-love motive in the unconscious, we become oppressed by a wearisome sense of premeditation and design, as if we were helpless in the cogs of a gigantic invisible machine; but when we look forward, from the dream to the future conduct of our life, we become inspired with the optimistic feeling

* " Collected Papers on Analytical Psychology," by C. G. Jung, M.D., LL.D., p. 222.

that the future lies in our own hands to fashion
as we please, by conscious design and the assistance of the mysterious operations of nature.
Freud does not lead us to a solution of our problems
of conduct, when he instructs us to conceive the
unconscious motive behind all human activity as
the desire for pleasure, and the aim of the unconscious as the immediate gratification of that desire
in thought or in deed, our dreams being a symbolic fulfilment to serve as a substitute in the
event of impracticability of fulfilment in act. But
Jung does, when he adds the constructive rider,
" What is the forward *purpose?* "   And, " To solve
some problem, and decide some unconscious conflict," is his reply. The psyche (or mind-activity)
is not, like the body, torpid during sleep, but is
busy achieving certain ends of its own, for this
purpose utilizing the primordial desires of the
unconscious; and so the dream-symbol plays some
part in the moral education of the individual, like
the religious symbol in the history of civilization.
Therefore, the dream symbol is to be interpreted,
not piecemeal in Freud's method, but as one big
symbol that perfectly represents the dreamer's
experience level and nervous tension at that
moment.

But Jung does not leave the central unconscious
motive entirely out of account; he pivots upon it
the individual's personality and love of life. For

the nervous state, he admits with Freud, is directly
dependent upon the unconscious which has
always one special tendency, " the ruling passion "
of Pope, which forms the ultimate source of satisfaction to the individual: when that tendency is
not frustrated, life is " worth living;" and what
that tendency is makes the man's personality this
or that. Bergson uses for it the term " élan vital,"
Freud the term " libido," or " interest."

Put in another way, " we have, as it were, a
number of instruments through which primal
energy runs. . . .   Behind them all lies the
same force . . . interest." The healthy-
minded man pours out his energy freely by all
the instruments, and not too much through one
and too little through another; he is, as we say,
" well balanced." The essential problem of a well-
regulated life is therefore that of how to ensure a
well-distributed flow of interest.

Open, unreserved people — the " impulsive "
type — have no difficulty in thus pouring out
their interest; they easily divert the current from
one channel to another; they act without much
forethought, and so it is men of this type that
perform the almost incredible feats of history.
Neither consistent nor thorough, they are yet able
to attract and fascinate an audience. Never
cautious nor matter-of-fact, they are seldom dull;
boldly imaginative, they make great actors, orators

and preachers. Their outpouring of interest is, however, in the extreme, too easy for a perfect balance.

The opposite type is close and reserved, meditation suits it rather than action, as it is suspicious of life, and expectant of disappointment. Such people have their interest dammed up, as it were; and though they are well aware themselves of an ardent inner life, they cannot reveal it to others, but give the impression of being cold, guarded, and difficult to understand. The extreme type is too ready to admit he is in the wrong, too sensitive to criticism, and too prone to make allowance for possible failure. " Suppose we fail," says the Macbeth of this type; but " Screw your courage to the sticking place, and we'll not fail," says the open Lady Macbeth.

Between the two extremes lies the balanced temperament, which is self-controlled, like the close type, but free in outlet, like the open. Dreams are a part of the nervous economy whose duty is it to maintain the balance. Thus Nebuchadnezzar, while at the height of his power dreamed* that a certain tree, which raised its head even up to the heavens, must now be hewn down. This was a symbol of abasement, which was a salutary reminder to a king with an exaggerated sense of his power.

* Daniel, Chap. IV.

" I am standing in a strange garden," runs the dream of a young man consulting a physician about his nerves, " and pluck an apple from a tree. I look about cautiously, to make sure no one sees me." Questioned about the origin of these particulars, the youth recollects that, years ago when he was quite a little boy, he had stolen a couple of pears from a garden; further, that on the day before the dream took place, he had been talking, more familiarly than he ought, to a certain girl, and that when a man had passed by whom he knew, he had turned away and looked shamefaced just the same as in the dream. Once, too, his father had chastised him for watching girls bathing; he had had a clandestine love affair, not yet broken off, with a housemaid; and his first association with an apple was that of the Fall, which he considered harshly unjust punishment, seeing that man's sin was a result of the character he had been born with.

The interpretation is obvious. The apple represents the youth's erotic desires; the embarrassed looking-round arises from the conflict between his conventional ideas and his acquired disdain for the Fall. Freud's theory would explain the dream as a fulfilment of the youth's wish for a fortunate termination to his love affair, disguised so as to evade his conscience which, though unsettled somewhat by acquired sophistries, is, through early training, sensitive to sexual sin. Jung's theory would explain that, through the skeptical company he keeps, the youth has formed a debased conception of sexual morality, superimposing upon the elevated one taught him by his father; but that in sleep he still conceives erotic desire as sin. The system of morality that he derides when he is awake is compensated for in his sleep by resuming its supremacy over him, on the principle that " those thoughts, propensities, and tendencies of a human personality which in conscious life are too seldom recognized, come spontaneously into action in the sleeping state, when to a large extent the conscious process is disconnected." The lesson of the dream, therefore, is that the young man should return in thought to the moral ideas of his childhood, and give up the immoral intrigues he is engaged in.

In contrast to this, a man of the noblest moral principles may have an immoral unconscious, as is shown by the temptations of St. Anthony; Saint Augustine even thanked God for His mercy in not holding him responsible for the sinfulness of his dreams.

" I am in a room in the midst of packing. I have to catch a train and the floor is littered with many things I want to pack. I cannot get them all into the trunk, and in a state of agitation I run out into the street. There is a great crowd of people outside, and I realize that it is hopeless to attempt to get to the station in time." Such is the dream occurring several times, recounted by an active woman of many interests, always organizing meetings and working to win recruits to a new movement.

To tell her that this is the fulfilment of an unconscious wish is not to help her a great deal, says Dr. Nicoll; but surely Freud's reading would be that the dreamer must either find a means to cope with the increasing burden of her work, or give up many of her activities — for the dream marks the desire to fulfil a task which is ever greater. Jung's scheme gives the same answer only in another form. There are too many things to pack, and there are too many people in the street: the dream symbolizes excess. The dreamer is giving out too much energy, and her plain duty to herself is to take a rest, and then reduce the program when she resumes work. Jung thus lays stress on the future; but by examining the past, Freud leads to the same conclusion, and gives the same advice in a slightly different form.

It is related by a writer of a book of travels how once he met with a native chief who always wore women's clothes. He learned that this man had once been a great and bloodthirsty warrior, but that, at the very height of his fame, after an expedition that had proved an unparalleled success, he had dreamed that the Great White Spirit had come to him, and bidden him from that time onwards be no longer a man, but a woman. The chief had thenceforward dressed like a woman and ordered his behavior on the model of the women of his tribe.

Freud would explain the dream as a longing for a peaceful life; Jung as a compensatory reaction after pouring out too much energy in bloodshed. The chief, by taking the warning literally, probably derived much satisfaction from his change of occupation, all the more so in that he turned an imaginary compensation into a real and active one.

In our own land a somewhat similar phenomenon often occurs, namely when elderly scientists who have devoted the best years of their life, and an excess of their energy to dry facts and materialistic theories, become thoroughly transformed into ardent spiritualists: it preserves their sanity, at the expense of their credit.

And so with dreams considered as wish fulfilments and as nervous compensations, we may draw the narrative to a close: we have reached the most enlightened views yet held on dreams, and those that will, in all likelihood, command the suffrages of the intelligent for many generations to come. In a different way, dreams, so much esteemed and regarded amongst the most primitive of races, are today as much esteemed and regarded by the most civilized of beings. They have come into their own again.

CHAPTER X

LITERATURE AS DREAMS

"We are all interested in the devil, because he is ourselves in our dreams and unguarded moments."

PSYCHO-ANALYSIS was first applied to literature in " The Interpretation of Dreams " (Traumdeutung), published in 1900, in which Freud gave his famous interpretation of the legend of King Œdipus; and the first book entirely devoted to the subject was also Freud's, namely, his analysis of Jensen's novel " Gradiva," in 1907. In spite of the recent date of both these books, already a great body of criticism has appeared, especially in America,* and more is constantly being done.

The general idea is that literary works are wish fulfilments in the Freudian sense, and compensatory activities in the Jungian sense, and in a manner organic products corresponding to dreams. Thus, the villains created by poets, dramatists and novelists, are compensatory reactions to the customary goodness of their lives, and the release of unconscious desires for evil;

* See " The Erotic Motive in Literature," by Albert Mondell (Boni and Liveright, New York, 1919).

Vautrin is part of Balzac's worse nature allowed rein in imagination, Mr. Hyde and John Silver are Stevenson's, Richard Varney is Scott's, Iago is Shakespeare's. So also do schoolboys obtain compensation for their dull routine of work in penny dreadfuls and blood-curdling films.

" Mr. Yeats in his last book of prose, put forward the suggestion that the artist reveals in his art not his ' self ' (which is expressed in his life), but his ' anti-self,' a complementary and even contrary self. He might find in the life and works of Meredith some support for his not quite convincing theory. Meredith was an egoist in his life, and anti-egoist in his books. He was pretentious in his life, anti-pretentious in his books. He took up the attitude of the wronged man in his life; he took up the case of the wronged woman in his books. In short, his life was vehemently pro-George-Meredith, while his books were vehemently anti-George-Meredith."* This is a clear case of compensation.

Balzac was very ambitious, and plunged into wild schemes for getting rich quick; and however moral his conscious ideas were, it is by no means unlikely that his unconscious would suggest to his mind that riches, fame, and love, might be obtained by breaking the merely human laws of honesty and justice. Thrusting back the sugges-

* " The Art of Letters," by Robert Lynd, 1920.

tion, as we would, he could not prevent its appearance in a disguised form in the portrayal of his characters. So Vautrin, in "Lost Illusions," endeavors to persuade Eugene to marry the heiress to a fortune of a million francs, and secure the inheritance at once by having her brother, the immediate claimant, secretly murdered.

"Do you believe," asks Vautrin, otherwise Balzac's unconscious, "that there is any absolute standard in the world? Despise mankind, and find out the meshes that you can slip through in the code." Balzac's resistance, that is, the censor, is given expression to by the words of Eugene, who shouts, "Silence, sir! I will not hear any more; you make me doubt myself."

Milton's unconscious obtains an outlet in Satan, Marlowe's (and also Goethe's) in Mephistopheles, the common people of the Middle Ages in the vice and devil of the morality plays. "We are all interested in the devil, because he is ourselves in our dreams and unguarded moments."

The unconscious, with his predilection for the part of villain, would, were he given full sway, make polite society and orderly civilization a thing impossible; but the moral sense succeeds very largely in keeping him in check — except in moments of distress and battle. The world carries on its activities by camouflaging the unconscious, for decency and charity's sake. "Men would not live long in society," runs one of La Rochefoucauld's maxims, " were they not the dupes of each other "; and he might well have added, of themselves.

Polite literature is equally dependent on the limitation and disguise of the unconscious but in reverse manner; it is a natural outlet for the anxiety neuroses of certain temperaments, induced by abstinence, repression, or unsatisfactory gratification of the love desire — as represented, for example by Hester Prynne, Madame Bovary, Hedda Gabler and Hamlet. Literature, writes Mr. Albert Mondell, taking an extreme and morbid view of the case, is " largely a record of the anxieties and hysterics of humanity." He confounds us with instances; thus he takes Byron's unfortunate love affair with his cousin Mary Chaworth, and shows how it is the motive for some fifty of his shorter poems, and that she is represented in " Manfred " as Astarte, and in " Don Juan " as Lady Adeline. Spenser's " Amoretti " (which is certainly true), he says, and Shakespeare's " Sonnets," are also the expression of disappointed love. But we may retort that even if this be so, the enjoyment of literature is also a safety valve for the anxieties and worries of readers.

According to this view, we like such books as " Robinson Crusoe," " Treasure Island," " Tarzan of the Apes," and the works of Scott, Dumas, Cooper, Gaboriau and Doyle, because we have not completely stripped off our ancestral robe of barbarism and boyhood, and the unconscious is therefore gratified by such tales. We are fascinated by marvels and mystery, and by accounts of what our ancestors did, like fishing, hunting and fighting. But a time comes when too many such books produce a sterility of exaggeration, when the heroes become too heroic, obedient to extravagant codes of honor, and triumphant over the impossible; and when the heroines become perfect beings, far above human frailties and impossibly beautiful; and when utopias are created that are too utopian in their disregard for our common human failings to command even a momentary belief; and then a reaction takes place, and during the next age, the public demand realistic novels, describing life as it is, and perferably in its sordid corners and under its most disgusting aspects — and we have an age of abnormal Zolaesque fiction. So do romanticism and realism take their turns in the development of literature in every country. It is again a system of compensation working.

But Freudian wish fulfilment is present equally with compensation; as we see in examining the working of the Œdipus Complex in literature, *i.e.*, the imaginative fulfilments of undirected parental affection. The normal development of affection, as has been shown already, is from love of the parent of the opposite sex, to love of a mate; and it is bad for the happiness of the individual if either is interrupted or if the transition from the one to the other is not easy. Examples of the nervous conflicts brought on by faultiness of early affections are common in literary history; and much work of outstanding importance has resulted from them.

Thus William Cowper's mother died when he was six years of age; but that his affection for her was lasting is shown by the poignant " Lines Written on the Receipt of my Mother's Picture," which was composed when he was fifty-eight. He did not marry. Mary Unwin was his mother-substitute, but not completely enough to heal the loss; and when he received his mother's picture, he kissed it, and hung it up where he could see it the last thing at night and the first thing in the morning. He describes his mother's tenderness, her nightly visits to tuck him in, her gifts of biscuits, her fond caresses; all was as vivid in his old age as if it had been but yesterday. This unhealthy attachment was never broken off, and, according to Freud's theory, it was the cause of his eccentricities and fits of despondency and madness.

Schopenhauer and Byron early in life quarrelled with their mothers; they became pessimists and cynics. Edgar Allan Poe and Lafcadio Hearn both lost their mothers in infancy; they became eccentric and morbid. Molière lost his mother early, and married unhappily; he was a sad man, with misanthropic moods. Thackeray had the like misfortune, added to which he loved where he could not marry; he was an unhappy man, disposed to cynicism. Ruskin was too devoted to a mother with stern ideas on work, his early love affair was unsuccessful and his marriage was unfortunate; he suffered continually from nervous breakdowns. But Robert Browning, who had a quiet normal affection for his mother, and who had a happy marriage, was a confirmed optimist.

An author, actuated by the unconscious, may reveal his private griefs in a disguised form, and repeat them again and again in his works. Charlotte Brontë, when at school in Brussels both as scholar and teacher, fell in love with the headmaster, M. Héger; as he was a married man, she suffered perpetual disappointment. So, writes Mrs. Chadwick, " The principal male characters to be found in Charlotte Brontë's novels were those drawn from M. Héger — M. Pelet, Rochester, Robert Moore, Louis Moore and Paul Emanuel." In fact it is the constant repetition of the theme of disappointed love that points to its real existence in the author herself.

Dickens' two love affairs were connected with

girls and not grown-up women, and so, as both were disappointing, he missed making a happy marriage, with its opportunities for learning the character of woman when fully developed; Maria Beadnell (Dora in " David Copperfield ") rejected him when a boy, and Mary Hogarth (Little Nell in " The Old Curiosity Shop "), his wife's younger sister, died very young. Mary Hogarth then served as his model for women, and it is for that reason that they are so bloodless and unindividualized, a mere " galaxy of amazing dolls variously dressed."

Literature is colored by the personality of its authors, and that in its turn depends upon the unconscious; and so, in many ways, creative literature may be said to be a product coördinate with dreams, and affording the same relief to the repressed desires of its creators. Like dreams, it is one of the many marvellous pieces of natural mechanism that render life tolerable under the artificial conditions of civilization; as Keats feverishly exclaimed,

" O, ease my heart of verse and let me rest."

CHAPTER XI

DREAMS IN LITERATURE

" My Brownies are somewhat fantastic, like their stories, hot and hot." — R. L. Stevenson, " Across the Plains."

HARDLY a long poem or story ever written but contains some reference to dreams, they are so well suited to convey a score of different ideas, or to hang an incident or fantasy upon. It would therefore be an endless and a futile task to take stock of the dream references even in our own language alone; a complete anthology would furnish out a library.

Dreams are, however, more commonly used for some purposes than for others; and it is proposed in this chapter to consider a few of them.

Shakespeare uses the word " dream " one hundred and fifty times altogether, the highest number in one play being nineteen, in " King Richard III." He used " dreamed " eighteen times, " dreamt " twelve, " dreaming " eight, " dreamer " four. Shelley is still more liberal: he gives us the noun " dream " more than one hundred and twenty times, and " dreams " ninety-eight times; the verb " dream " forty-two

times; " dreamed " twelve, " dreaming " twenty,
and " dreamer " four times. Tennyson uses
" dream " or " dreams " as a noun one
hundred and sixty-three times, and as a verb
fifty-two times; " dream'd " and " dreamt " occur
thirty-eight times, " dreaming " fifteen and
" dreamer " five.

Occurring with such frequency, " dream " and
its derivatives have developed many fresh meanings, all connected with the notion of something
insubstantial, transitory, prophetic and ideal.
" To Live But in a Dreame of Friendship "*
conveys the notion of an illusory state; and idle
speculation is the meaning in " The dreams of
Rabelais's commentators have indeed discovered
a very difficult intention."† Emerson sometimes
used " dream " in the sense of visionary anticipa-
tion — " The search after the great is the dream
of youth ";‡ Hawthorne as the ideal — " London
the dream-city of my youth ";§ Tennyson as to
hover over drowsily —

"As when the sun, a crescent of eclipse,
Dreams over lake and lawn," ‖ and

Shakespeare as to have some conception of —

" There are more things in Heaven and Earth, Horatio
Than are dream't of in your Philosophy."¶

* " Timon of Athens," IV, ii, 34.
† Ferriar, " Illustrated Sterne," ii, 24; in 1798.
‡ " Representative Men," Bohn, I, 274; 1847.
§ " Our Old Home," 240; 1863.
‖ " Vision of Sin," 11; 1842.
¶ " Hamlet," I, v, 168; 1602.

In Hall's Chronicles* " dream " is used in the meaning of " to act indolently," — " He mindyng no longer to dreame in his waightie matter nor to kepe secrete his right and title "; and a writer in the " Daily News "† meant by it "something uncommonly charming," — " Attired in a succession of those lovely gowns which enthusiasts delight to describe as a ' dream '." And this does not exhaust the possible meanings.

As a simile, as well as metaphorically, it has been used a myriad of times, and often magnificently. Memorable examples occur in the Old Testament scriptures. " And the multitude of all the nations that fight against Israel . . . ," say verses 7 and 8 of Isaiah, Chapter 29, " shall be as a dream of a night vision. It shall even be as when an hungry man dreameth, and, behold, he eateth; but he awaketh, and his soul is empty; or as when a thirsty man dreameth, and, behold, he drinketh; but he awaketh, and, behold, he is faint, and his soul hath appetite: so shall the multitude of all the nations be, that fight against mount Zion." Zophar the Naamathite cried,‡ " He shall fly away as a dream, and shall not be found: yea, he shall be chased away as a vision of the night."

We ourselves, in Prospero's solemn adjuration, " are such stuff as dreams are made on." And a

* " Henry VI," vi, 1626; 1548.
† 2 May, 1892, 2/1.
‡ Job, 20, 8.

" dreamer," is a man that fritters away his life in unprofitable speculations: " He is a dreamer, let us leave him."[*]

Innumerable essays have appeared under the title, Dreams, by great authors as well as others. Lending itself equally well to philosophic disquisition or to play of fancy, it suits Hazlitt equally with Lamb; and as a framework or pretext for story-telling, as in " Alice in Wonderland," it has few equals. It permits of more license than the story-telling devices of " The Decameron" and the " Canterbury Tales," though it is scarcely of the same service for realistic purposes; and how familiar is such a beginning of a tale as, " He had been reading ' Don Quixote ' by the seaside; and, oppressed by the heat of the sun, he had fallen asleep, whilst gazing on the barren sand before him. . . . He dreams that, walking in some sandy wilderness of Africa, some endless Sahara, he sees at a distance

> 'An Arab of the desert, lance in rest,
> Mounted upon a dromedary.' "[†]

And the ending, too: " whereat I waked in terror,

> And saw the sea before me, and the book
> In which I had been reading at my side."

Sir Thomas Browne's essay " Of Dreams," is a quaint mixture of naïveté and practicality. " How-

[*] De Quincey's " Reminiscences of the Lake Poets."
[†] " Julius Caesar," L, ii, 24.

ever dreams may be fallacious concerning outward events," he acutely if mistakenly remarked, "yet may they be truly significant at home; and whereby we may more sensibly understand ourselves. Men act in sleep with some conformity unto their awaked senses; and consolations or discouragements may be drawn from dreams which intimately tell us ourselves. Luther was not like to fear a spirit of the night, when such an apparition would not terrify him in the day. Alexander would hardly have run away in the sharpest combats of sleep, nor Demosthenes have stood stoutly to it, who was scarce able to do it in his prepared senses. Persons of radical integrity will not easily be perverted in their dreams, nor noble minds do pitifully things in sleep. Cassius would hardly have been bountiful in a dream, whose fist was so close awake. But a man might have lived all his life upon the sleeping hand of Antonius."

More acutely and more truly, Owen Feltham, a contemporary of Browne's, in another essay " Of Dreams," says " Dreams are notable means of discovering our own inclinations. The wise man learns to know himself as well by the night's black mantle, as the searching beams of day. In sleep we have the naked and natural thoughts of our souls: outward objects interpose not, either to shuffle in occasional cogitations, or bale out the included fancy. Surely, how we fall to vice, or rise to virtue, we may by observation find in our dreams. The best use we can make of dreams, is observation and by that, our own correction or encouragement. For 'tis not doubtable, but that the mind is working in the dullest depth of sleep."

At the beginning of the nineteenth century Hazlitt shot a bolt still nearer to the truth; in some ways, he is, indeed, the forerunner of Freud. " There is a sort of profundity in sleep," runs the essay " On Dreams " in " The Plain Speaker "; " it may be said that the voluntary power is suspended, and things come upon us as unexpected revelations, which we keep out of our thoughts at other times. We may be aware of a danger that we do not choose, while we have the full command of our faculties, to acknowledge to ourselves; the impending event will then appear to us as a dream, and we shall most likely find it verified afterwards. Another thing of no small consequence is, that we may sometimes discover our tacit and almost *unconscious* sentiments, with respect to persons or things in the same way. We are not hypocrites in our sleep. The curb is taken off from our passions and our imagination wanders at will. When awake, we check these rising thoughts, and fancy we have them not. In dreams when we are off our guard, they return securely and unbidden. We make this use of the infirmity of our sleeping metamorphoses, that we may *repress* any feelings of this sort that we disapprove in their incipient state, and detect, ere it be too late, an unwarrantable antipathy or fatal passions. Infants cannot disguise their thoughts from others; and in sleep we reveal the secret to ourselves." Italics are our own.

Charles Lamb, about the same time, wrote of his own personal dream experiences in childhood. Those he describes are not normal — or why should he trouble us with their recital — but that is characteristic of the dreams recounted in literature. It is in " Witches, and Other Night Fears " that he relates how deeply he was affected as a child by the gaudy illustrations in Stackhouse's " History of the Bible," a copy of which stood in the family bookcase. He was fascinated by the picture of " The Witch raising up Samuel." However, as he poked his finger through the elephant and camel in the Ark, his father took the book from him and locked it securely away; vivid images of it then haunted the child's mind in sleep.

" I never," he continues, " laid my head on my pillow, I suppose, from the fourth to the seventh or eighth year of my life without an assurance, which realized its own prophecy, of seeing some frightful spectre. . . . It was he (Stackhouse) who dressed up for me a hag that nightly sate upon my pillow — a sure bedfellow, when my aunt or my maid was far from me." As he grew up, the nightmares ceased. "My night-fancies," he now avers, "have long ceased to be afflictive. I confess an occasional nightmare; but I do not, as in early youth, keep a stud of them." His usual adult dreams "are never romantic, seldom even rural. They are of architecture and buildings — cities abroad, which I have never seen and hardly have hoped to see. I have traversed for the seeming length of a natural day, Rome, Amsterdam, Paris, Lisbon — their churches, palaces, squares, market-places, shops, suburbs, ruins, with an inexpressible sense of delight — a map-like distinctness of trace, and a daylight vividness of vision, that was all but being awake." The reader will have formed his own conclusion of the meaning of such dreams as these; Lamb the Londoner, certainly cared nothing for the Lakes, but liked cities, which he visited in his dreams.

"The poverty of my dreams," he added, thinking of Coleridge's resplendent visions, "mortifies me." After reading Barry Cornwall's dream of nereids and tritons, Lamb too dreamed of the sea, with himself as principal god at some maritime nuptials, but the effort was too great for him, soon the billows subsided into wavelets, the sea waned first into a lake and then into a river, which he recognized as the Thames; and it "landed me in the wafture of a placid wave or two, alone, safe and inglorious, somewhere at the foot of Lambeth Palace."

He goes on, in a later part of the essay, to attribute dreams to the fancy and imagination: " The degree of the soul's creativeness in sleep might furnish no whimsical criterion of the quantum of poetical faculty resident in the same soul waking. An old gentlemen, a friend of mine, and a humorist, used to carry this notion so far, that when he saw any stripling of his acquaintance ambitious of becoming a poet, his first question would be, ' Young man, what sort of dreams have you?' I have so much faith in my old friend's theory that when I feel that idle vein returning upon me, I presently subside into my proper element of prose, remembering those eluding nereids, and that inauspicious inland landing."

" The newly married woman," wrote MacNish in a significant passage, " conceives herself (in dreams) to be encircled by children, and experiencing intense pleasure in their innocent society. Men who are very fond of children often experience the same sensations and both men and women who are naturally indifferent in this respect, seldom dream about them, and never with any feelings of peculiar delight." In view of this, a particular interest attaches to the delightful sketch that Lamb, the bachelor, gives us, in " Dream-Children: a Reverie," of one of his dreams. " My little ones

crept about me," he begins, " the other evening
to hear about their great-grandmother Field, who
lived in a great house in Norfolk." When they
heard her described, John smiled, and Alice's little
right foot played an involuntary movement; and
when they heard about the death of their uncle
John, a spirited youth, they began to weep, and
begged him to stop and tell them about their
mother. " Then I told how for seven long years,
in hope sometimes, sometimes in despair, yet
persisting ever, I courted the fair Alice W——n;
when suddenly turning to Alice, the soul of the
first Alice looked out of her eyes with such a
reality of re-presentment, that I became in doubt
which of them stood there before me, or whose
that bright hair was; and while I stood gazing,
both the children gradually grew fainter to my
view, receding, and still receding, till nothing
at last but two mournful features were seen in
the uttermost distance, which, without speech,
strangely impressed upon me the effects of speech:
'We are not of Alice, nor of thee, nor are we
children at all. The children of Alice call Bartrum
father. We are nothing; less than nothing, and
dreams. We are only what might have been, and
must wait upon the tedious shores of Lethe
millions of ages before we have existence, and a
name,' — and immediately awaking, I found
myself quietly seated in my bachelor armchair,

where I had fallen asleep, with the faithful Bridget unchanged by my side."

Yet another essayist of that age was a dreamer. For fourteen years, Thomas de Quincey was an opium eater; and his "Confessions" contain descriptions, written in his ample swelling prose, of the extraordinary dreams induced by the practice. Once, while staying in Cumberland, a Malay — the last extreme of the unexpected in the still unknown and secluded Lake District — had knocked at the door of his cottage; and De Quincey had been so affected by the contrast between this man and his surroundings, that he had conceived in the instant a predilection for the East: the consequence was that a number of his dreams carried him to the Malay Archipelago and China, where he saw vivid images of gorgeous scenery and horrid tortures. " I was," he tells us, " stared at, hooted at, grinned at, chattered at, by monkeys, by paroquets, by cockatoos. Thousands of years I lived and was buried in stone coffins, with mummies and sphinxes. I was kissed with cancerous kisses by crocodiles."

A close August, with not a breath of wind, making a powerful impression on De Quincey's thoughts, which turned persistently to the subject of death, he began to dream of being in Judea, where, under palm-trees, a girl was sitting on a stone; and that girl was Ann, who, abandoned herself had yet taken pity on the boyish De Quincey on his first and solitary arrival in London, and who, after he had conceived feelings of the deepest gratitude to her, had suddenly and inexplicably disappeared. He had searched high and low for her; and part of this dream expresses his warm desire to find her. Thoughts of religion, death and affection are mingled in the symbolism of the dream.

De Quincey had been wont in early childhood, like other very imaginative children, to paint (as it were) before his inward eye, as he was falling off to sleep, whatever phantom images were prompted to his mind by the mood he was in; and these instantly flashed before him as vivid and real as dreams. At the beginning, when these experiences had not become habitual, he could evoke or dismiss the images at his pleasure; but as time went on, they gained the upper hand over him, and persisted right on into his sleep, when they assumed what form they liked. The result was that he became haunted by visions of vast processions moving along interminably with mournful pomp, while no efforts of his would suffice to stop them; and the phantoms that flitted before his mind awake reappeared in his sleep with a splendor insufferable.

In adult life, he began the opium habit, with immediate effect on his dreams; buildings and landscapes affected him with a sense of overpowering vastness, and a single night seemed protracted into a century. The minutest details of his childhood, completely forgotten while he was awake, were revived in his dreams with startling vividness; the Livy that he had once been fond of reappeared in the person of Paullus and Marius, and in the dread pronouncement by a solemn voice of " Consul Romanus," the Civil Wars of the reign of Charles I, in which he had once delighted, reappeared in the form of beautiful Cavalier ladies.

As years went on, the dreams altered their form. He had visions of elaborate masses of architecture, expanding continually before his eyes; and of never-ending expanses of silvery lakes. Then ensued horrible nightmares: " the sea was paved with innumerable faces, upturned to the heavens; faces imploring, wrathful, despairing," reminding him somehow — here one sees the wish-fulfilment element — of long-vanished Ann. Not all the dreams, though, were visual. He heard tumultuous noises, " with a music such as now I often heard in sleep, the undulations of fast-gathering tumults, the tread of innumerable armies," ending up with a terrific crash in mid-air. At times he experienced a feeling of helpless rigidity, like a Ferdinand charmed by Prospero: " I (as usual in dreams where, of necessity, we make ourselves central to every movement) had the power, and yet had not the power, to decide it . . . the weight of twenty Atlantics was upon me."

" When the dream binds him that he cannot rise."*

De Quincey at last succeeded in withstanding the temptation of opium, his dreams resumed their normal form and here the record stops.

Yet another kind of dream, not merely fanciful like Lamb's, nor yet induced by drugs, fell to the lot of R. L. Stevenson, who gives an interesting account of them in " Across the Plains "†: it is the dream creative. Like Lamb R. L. Stevenson " was from a child an ardent and uncomfortable dreamer," afflicted by painful nightmares. "When he had a touch of fever at night, and the room swelled and shrank, and his clothes, hanging on a nail, now loomed up instant to the bigness of a church, and now drew away into a horror of infinite distance and infinite littleness, the poor soul was very well aware of what must follow, and struggled hard against the approaches of that slumber which was the beginning of sorrows. But his struggles were in vain; sooner or later the night-hag would have him by the throat, and pluck him, strangling and screaming, from his sleep. His dreams were at times commonplace enough, at times very strange: at times they were

* " Enslaved," by John Masefield.
† Chapter VIII.

almost formless, he would be haunted, for instance,
by nothing more definite than a certain hue of
brown, which he did not mind in the least while
he was awake, but feared and loathed while he
was dreaming; at times, again, they took on every
detail of circumstance, as when once he supposed
he must swallow the populous world, and awoke
screaming with the horror of the thought. The
two chief troubles of his very narrow existence —
the practical and everyday struggle of school
tasks and the ultimate and airy one of hell and
judgment — were often confounded together into
one appalling nightmare. He seemed to himself
to stand before the Great White Throne; he was
called on, poor little devil, to recite some form of
words, on which his destiny depended; his tongue
stuck, his memory was blank, hell gaped for him;
and he would awake, clinging to the curtain-rod
with his knees to his chin."

The time came when such contortions ceased,
"and he would awake with no more extreme
symptom than a flying heart, a freezing scalp,
cold sweats, and the speechless midnight fear ";
and a later development succeeded, when his
dreams became quite normal, but continuous and
convincing like life itself. " The look of the world
beginning to take hold on his attention, scenery
came to play a part in his sleeping as well as in
his waking thoughts, so that he would take long,

uneventful journeys, and see strange towns and
beautiful places as he lay in bed. And, what is
more significant, an odd taste that he had for the
Georgian costume and for stories laid in that
period of English history, began to rule the features
of his dreams; so that he masqueraded there in a
three-cornered hat, and was much engaged with
Jacobite conspiracy between the hour for bed and
that for breakfast. About the same time he began
to read in his dreams — tales for the most part,
and for the most part after the manner of G. P. R.
James, but so incredibly more vivid and moving
than any printed book, that he has been ever
since malcontent with literature.

" And then, while he was yet a student, there
came to him a dream-adventure which he has no
anxiety to repeat; he began, that is to say, to
dream in sequence and thus to lead a double life—
one of the day, one of the night. . . . I should
have said he studied . . . at Edinburgh College.
. . . Well, in his dream-life, he passed a long day
in the surgical theatre, his heart in his mouth,
his teeth on edge, seeing monstrous malformations
and the abhorred dexterity of surgeons. In a
heavy, rainy, foggy evening he came forth into
the South Bridge, turned up the High Street, and
entered the door of a tall *land*, at the top of which
he supposed himself to lodge. All night long, in
his wet clothes, he climbed the stairs, stair after

stair in endless series, and at every second flight a flaming lamp with a reflector. All night long, he brushed by single persons passing downward — beggarly women of the street, great, weary, muddy labourers, poor scarecrows of men, pale parodies of women — but all drowsy and weary like himself, and all single, and all brushing against him as they passed. In the end, out of a northern window, he would see day beginning to whiten over the Firth, give up the ascent, turn to descend, and in a breath be back again upon the streets, in his wet clothes, in the wet, haggard dawn, trudging to another day of monstrosities and operations. Time went quicker in the life of dreams, some seven hours (as near as he can guess) to one; and it went, besides, more intensely, so that the gloom of these fancied experiences clouded the day, and he had not shaken off their shadow ere it was time to lie down and to renew them."

He consulted a doctor, whose advice enabled him to get rid of the complaint, and become a normal dreamer; yet from time to time his dreams contained all the elements of the plot of a story, which he conceived the notion of writing for publication. Lying in bed, he would plunge into a tale — a mere succession of hairbreadth escapes and thrilling adventures, like " Gil Blas," or " Don Quixote " — hoping that some of them would last into his sleep, and give rise to others. " When he lay down to prepare himself for sleep, he no longer sought amusement, but printable profitable tales; and after he had dozed off in his box-seat, his little people continued their evolutions with the same mercantile designs." Other dreams then stopped altogether. " He would wake up crying, ' I have it, that'll do! ' " Sometimes the tales were not of the right sort, while others surpassed what he could invent awake; he then awarded the honor of invention not to himself, but to his " Brownies," who did the hard work for him, leaving little to do but write them up, prepare the manuscript for the press, and pay for registering the packet in the post.

The two stories the Brownie origin of which he enlarges upon are " Olalla," a somewhat feeble effort, and the popular success, " Dr. Jekyll and Mr. Hyde."

" Olalla " is contained in the collection of tales entitled " The Merry Men," and is a study of the degeneration of an aristocratic Spanish family through close intermarriage. A wounded British officer was lodged for his period of convalescence in the house of a proud but decayed family in a country town of Spain; the decay was marked by taking in a lodger for profit, and the pride by the stipulation made when he was accepted, namely, that there should be no intercourse between him and the household. There were two children, of

very opposite disposition, the boy Felipe being
stupid and boorish, and the girl Olalla clever and
dignified; while their mother — of whom he caught
a glimpse one day sitting in the courtyard — was
good-looking but half lunatic.

One night, horrible shrieks resounding through
the house, the officer tried to find out what was
the cause, but in vain. Next day, he made a strict
search, and penetrated at last to a tastefully fur-
nished room, littered with books and papers,
composing, he did not doubt, Olalla's study,
though she was not there herself.

Another day he met her on the stairs, and, for
she was very beautiful, he fell head over ears
in love with her; at first she gave him some encouragement, but later ordered him to leave the house.
He was reluctant to go, and her mother, in a fit
of madness, springing on him and biting his hand
badly, he stayed and was nursed by Olalla, whom
he now confidently hoped to win; and very soon
he got well again. But now Olalla spoke out, and
bade him depart forever. She had made a vow—
not to be shaken even by her love for him — to
end her family with herself, because it was irre-
mediably degenerate. She would die single rather
than run the risk of bearing degenerate children.

Quitting the house, in obedience to her orders,
he went into the neighboring mountains and stayed
there in a village which Olalla was likely to visit

from time to time. Finally she appeared and he obtained the interview he had hoped for — the last, as he found; for she gave him her final decision, namely, to keep single all her life, and she bade him, in fairness to her, to go away altogether and not try to see her again.

It is a melancholy, unsatisfactory story, with an unreal air, strained characterization, and humorless situations. A tedious introduction, long and unnecessary descriptive passages, and an unconvincing plot, make it dull reading. It is a feverish exotic fantasm, like a bad dream.

This "not very defensible story" came into existence in the following way:

" The count, the mother, the mother's uncle, Olalla, Olalla's chamber, the meetings on the stair, the broken window, the ugly scene of the bite, were all given me in bulk and detail as I have tried to write them; to this I added only the external scenery (for in my dream I never was beyond the court), the portrait, the characters of Felipe and the priest, the moral, such as it is, and the last pages, such as, alas! they are. And I may even say that in this case the moral itself was given me for it arose immediately on a comparison of the mother and the daughter, and from the hideous trick of atavism in the first. Sometimes a parabolic sense is still more undeniably present in a dream; sometimes I cannot but suppose my

Brownies have been aping Bunyan, and yet in no case with what would possibly be called a moral in a tract; never with the ethical narrowness; conveying hints instead of life's larger limitations. For the most part, it will be seen, my Brownies are somewhat fantastic, like their stories hot and hot, full of passion, and the picturesque, alive with animating incident; and they have no prejudice against the supernatural."

Stevenson adds the definite touches of observation to the vague original presented by the dream. The niche becomes " a certain pillared recess, which bore the marks of human habitation "; Olalla's chamber " was of large proportions and faced to the north; the embers of a fire smoldered and smoked upon the hearth, to which a chair had been drawn close; the floor and walls were naked; books of all sorts, devotional, historical and scientific, but mostly of a great age and in the Latin tongue," Olalla " glowed in the deep shadow of the gallery, a gem of colour."

More graphic, sudden, and dream-like are the incidents. " I went very lightly across the court and up the marble staircase. My foot was on the topmost round, when a door opened, and I found myself face to face with Olalla. Surprise transfixed me; her loveliness struck to my heart." As vivid is the incident of the bite. " And then, like one in a dream, I moved to the window, put forth my hand to open the casement, and thrust it through the pane. The blood spouted from my wrist.

" ' I have cut myself,' I said, ' and rather badly. See! ' and I held out my two hands from which the blood was oozing and dripping. Her (the mother's) great eyes opened wide, the pupils shrank into points; she came swiftly up to me, and stooped and caught me by the hand; and the next moment my hand was at her mouth, and she had bitten me to the bone."

" The Strange Case of Dr. Jekyll and Mr. Hyde " is a story of double personality, told by Mr. Utterson, Dr. Jekyll's lawyer friend. Dr. Jekyll, a wealthy and highly respected physician, had made a will leaving his fortune, contrary to all expectations, to one Edward Hyde, a scoundrel who possessed a mysterious influence over him. Hyde was " pale and dwarfish; he gave an impression of deformity without any namable malformation, he had a displeasing smile; and he spoke with a husky whispering and somewhat broken voice." Utterson once caught Hyde stealing into Dr. Jekyll's disused dissecting room, and a year later he heard that Hyde had murdered Sir Danvers Carew, by felling him with a loaded stick. After this, when pressed by his friends, Dr. Jekyll took an oath that he would never see Hyde again; and for a time he kept his promise and became as sociable as he had been before Hyde's advent.

However, one Sunday afternoon, while taking a stroll past Jekyll's house, Utterson, seeing the doctor at the window, and beginning a conversation with him from the street, suddenly saw " the smile struck out of his face and succeeded by an expression of such abject terror and despair as froze the very blood of the gentleman below."

Some days later Dr. Jekyll's servant Poole called on Mr. Utterson and told him that the doctor had locked himself in a cabinet a week ago, and refusing to come out when called upon, had resisted every effort of the servants to get at him. Every night they had heard some one pacing to and fro in his room and they suspected that it might be Hyde, who had murdered the doctor and taken his place. Utterson repaired directly to Jekyll's, and with the assistance of the servants, broke down the door of the cabinet and discovered — the body of Hyde, " sorely contorted still and twitching," he having committed suicide by taking kernels. The doctor was nowhere to be seen, but it was presumed that he was dead.

Mr. Utterson now felt entitled to open a sealed packet that the doctor had placed in his keeping on the understanding that it was to be opened only in an emergency; and he there read, with surprise and horror, Dr. Jekyll's own account of the mysterious transactions.

Jekyll's confession began by explaining that very early in life, through having strong tendencies simultaneously to both good and evil, he had been driven to practice constant duplicity. Afterwards he had formed a theory, which he had ardently believed, that man has a double personality; and he had conceived that by experiment he might discover some means of isolating the two selves. At last he had succeeded; he had found a chemical which would enable him to assume one personality alone at a time. He took a dose of the mixture, which contained a certain salt, and almost immediately, feeling a deadly nausea and racking pains all over his body, he was transformed into a new personality, consisting of his own evil self, separated from his good self, and visible to the world as one Mr. Edward Hyde.

In order to change back into Dr. Jekyll, he had to drink an antidote; then he became once more the compound of good and evil that he had originally been — he did not change into his solely-good self. With practice he grew so accustomed to the transformation that he hardly feared it; and in his other person he began to commit atrocious crimes, and yet escape detection. As Dr. Jekyll he remembered the crimes he had committed, but he felt no remorse on their account, as they were Hyde's affair, not his.

One morning, however, when Dr. Jekyll got

up he saw in the glass that he had become Mr. Hyde automatically in his sleep. Realizing at last the dreadful peril of the course he was following, Jekyll made a gallant effort to abstain from the drug; but once falling in a moment of weakness, he undid the good of all his efforts by savagely murdering the famous physician, Sir Danvers Carew. Automatic transformations redoubled in frequency; and worse still, he found his supply of the antidote fast giving out. The climax arrived when he discovered that the new salt ordered for the antidote mixture was pure and contained none of the accidental but essential ingredients of his former supplies; he could now no longer hope ever to recover his Dr. Jekyll personality.

His fate sealed, for he was as Edward Hyde wanted by the police, he locked himself away in his cabinet, drank his last dose of the thaumaturgic antidote, wrote down and sealed up his full confession, and then met his end as Edward Hyde, the murderer.

Such is the story in outline, a species of parable on the Freudian conscious and unconscious; its genesis was as follows: For a long time Stevenson had been toying with the idea of a story based on man's double self, and one attempt he had written out, namely, " The Travelling Companion," which had been rejected by a publisher. " For two days," he says, " I went about racking my brains for a plot of any sort; and on the second night I dreamed the scene at the window, and a scene afterwards split in two, in which Hyde, pursued for some crime, took the powder and underwent the change in the presence of his pursuers. All the rest was made awake, and consciously, although I think I can trace in much of it the manner of my Brownies. The meaning of the tale is therefore mine, and had long pre-existed in my garden of Adonis, and tried one body after another in vain; indeed, I do most of the morality, worse luck! and my Brownies have not a rudiment of what we call a conscience. Mine, too, is the setting, mine the characters. All that was given me was the matter of three scenes, and the central idea of a voluntary change becoming involuntary." The critics must reserve their censure of these last things and certain other things too, for the Brownies; thus " the business of the powders, which so many have censured, is, I am relieved to say, not mine at all but the Brownies." Still, Stevenson is responsible for most of the tale; he provided the setting, the house, rooms, door, cabinet, and dissecting room; the characters of Utterson, his friend Enfield, Jekyll's old friend Dr. Lanyon (who dies of heart failure when the horrible secret is confided to him), the old servant Poole, the Soho landlady, and Dr. Jekyll; and the moral, that evil indulged in will finally become our master.

The Brownies' sin is the provision of a dehuman-
ized atmosphere. The story contains no humor,
but an air of strained feverish unreality; it seems
machine-like and remote, like a mathematical
problem — interesting, very, but not like life.
Thus both of Stevenson's dream-generated short
stories are limited by what they work in; they
have the fantastic and intriguing qualities of the
dream, but also its unwholesome partiality; they
are products of the night. But, of course, Stevenson
is not the only story dreamer on record.*

The composition of verse, too, in dreams is
quite common, the classical example being Coleridge's fragment, " Kubla Khan," which the poet
modestly published " rather as a psychological
curiosity, than on the ground of any supposed
poetic merits." " In the summer of 1797, the
Author, then in ill health, had retired to a lonely
farmhouse between Porlock and Linton, on the
Exmoor confines of Somerset and Devonshire.
In consequence of slight indisposition, an anodyne
had been prescribed, from the effects of which he
fell asleep in his chair at the moment that he was
reading the following sentence, or words of the
same substance, in ' Purchas' Pilgrimage ': ' Here
the Khan Kubla commanded a palace to be built,
and a stately garden thereunto; and thus ten

---

* See " Dreams and Dream Stories," by Anna Lewis Kingsford
(edited by Edward Maitland), 1888, for numerous stories and poems
composed in sleep and recollected next day.

miles of fertile ground were inclosed with a wall.'
The author continued for about three hours in a
profound sleep, at least of the external senses,
during which time he had the most vivid confidence, that he could not have composed less than
from two to three hundred lines; if that indeed
can be called composition in which all the images
rose up before him as *things*, with a parallel production of the correspondent expressions, without
any sensation or consciousness of effort. On awaking he appeared to himself to have a distinct recollection of the whole, and taking his pen, ink, and
paper, instantly and eagerly wrote down the lines
that are here preserved. At this moment he was
unfortunately called out by a person on business
from Porlock, and detained by him above an
hour, and on his return to his room, found to his
no small surprise and mortification, that though
he still retained some vague and dim recollection
of the general purport of the vision, yet, with
the exception of some eight or ten scattered lines
and images, all the rest had passed away like the
images on the surface of a stream into which a
stone has been cast, but, alas! without the after-
restoration of the latter. . . . Yet from the still
surviving recollections in his mind, the author
has frequently purposed to finish for himself what
had been originally, as it were, given to him . . .
but the tomorrow has yet to come."

The poem, it will be readily seen, is fantastic in conception and liquid in metrical form. The sea is sunless and lifeless, the poet, were he to revive the Abyssinian maid's song within him, would be in a state of ecstasy, half mad, half divine; mysterious voices are borne on the air; the tumult of the waters is " as if this earth in fast thick pants were breathing "; this is the dream-state unmistakably with its phantasms " hot and hot." The language is singularly well chosen to produce an effect at once of music and suggestion: " ancestral voices prophesying war " is a touchstone of romantic expression. The harmony of waking composition, the construction of a waking romance, the definiteness of a waking description, are not here. We may certainly take Coleridge's word for it that the fragment was conceived and composed in a dream.

" In Xanadu did Kubla Khan
A stately pleasure-dome decree:
Where Alph, the sacred river, ran
Through caverns measureless to man
Down to a sunless sea.
So twice five miles of fertile ground
With walls and towers were girdled round:
And here were gardens bright with sinuous rills,
Where blossomed many an incense-bearing tree;
And here were forests ancient as the hills,
Enfolding sunny spots of greenery.
But oh! that deep romantic chasm that slanted
Down the green hill athwart a cedarn cover!

A savage place! as holy and enchanted
As e'er beneath a waning moon was haunted
By woman wailing for her demon-lover! . . .
And from this chasm, with ceaseless turmoil seething,
As if this earth in fast thick pants were breathing,
A mighty fountain momently was forced:
And mid the dancing rocks at once and ever
It flung up momently the sacred river.
Five miles meandering with a mazy motion
Through wood and dale the sacred river ran,
Then reached the caverns measureless to man,
And sank in tumult to a lifeless ocean:
And 'mid this tumult Kubla heard from far
Ancestral voices prophesying war! . . .
    A damsel with a dulcimer
    In a vision once I saw:
    It was an Abyssinian maid,
    And on her dulcimer she played,
    Singing of Mount Abora.
    Could I revive within me
    Her symphony and song,
    To such a deep delight 'twould win me,
That with music loud and long,
I would build that dome in air,
That sunny dome! Those caves of ice!
And all who heard should see them there,
And all should cry, Beware! Beware!
His flashing eyes, his floating hair!
Weave a circle round them thrice,
And close your eyes with holy dread,
For he on honey-dew hath fed,
And drank the milk of Paradise."

Mr. A. C. Benson's poem " The Phoenix " was written in much the same way, but it escaped the opium-fumes of " Kubla Khan," and has more construction and form. " I dreamed the whole poem in a dream, in 1894 I think, and wrote it down in the middle of the night on a scrap of paper by my bedside. I have never had a similar experience, and, what is more curious, it is a lyric of a style which I have never attempted before or since . . . . I really can offer no explanation either of the idea of the poem or its interpretation. It came to me so (apparently) without any definite volition of my own that I don't profess to understand or be able to interpret the symbolism."

The poem, of four quatrain verses, relates how the phoenix, the fabulous Arabian bird that lived sole, without mate, flew away to die by fire in the sacred place of the desert, and how then a new bird arose from the ashes of the old. The poem is sensuous, rich in musical sound, and bright with jewelled words; and in common with "Kubla Khan," it possesses some touch of eastern magic, like a dream-essence. (It will be noticed that in each verse the third line does not rhyme with the first, but the first and third lines contain internal rhymes.)

" By feathers green, across Casbeen,
    The pilgrims track the Phoenix flown,
By gems he strewed in waste and wood
    And jewelled plumes at random thrown.

Till wandering far, by moon and star,
    They stand beside the fruitful pyre,
Whence breaking bright with sanguine light,
    The impulsive bird forgets his sire.

Those ashes shine like ruby wine,
  Like bag of Tyrian murex spilt;
The claw, the jowl of the flying fowl
  Are with the glorious anguish gilt.

So rare the light, so rich the sight,
  Those pilgrim men, on profit bent,
Drop hands and eyes and merchandise,
  And are with gazing most content."

The static ending, "And are with gazing most content," is typical of a dream; and so are the gaudy colors, green, ruby, purple, gilt, blood-color: the dream-mood is the exotic mood, and some poets, like Francis Thompson, seem to dream awake.

In the drama, dreams are a useful alternative device to soliloquy, for exposing a character's inmost thoughts, without unnaturalness. A dream of this sort is always made obviously significant, either to foretell future events, or to symbolize the forces at work in the drama; and it is a very effective mode of revelation, because of its naturalness and its tendency to heighten the intensity of the emotions — thoughts and prophecies that have sunk into the soul even in sleep, have an air of being predestined and supernatural. It is a favorite device of Shakespeare's to introduce dreams of this kind.

Cleopatra: You laugh when boys or women tell their dreams;
        Is't not your trick?
Dolabella: I understand not, madam.

Cleopatra: I dream'd there was an emperor Antony:
        O, such another sleep, that I might see
        But such another man!
Dolabella: If it might please you, —
Cleopatra: His face was as the heavens; and therein stuck
        A sun and moon, which kept their course, and
          lighted
        The little O, the earth.
Dolabella: Most sovereign creature, —
Cleopatra: His legs bestrid the ocean: his rear'd army
        Crested the world: his voice was propertied
        As all the tuned spheres, and that to friends:
        But when he meant to quail and shake the orb,
        He was as rattling thunder. For his bounty,
        There was no winter in't: in his livery
        Walk'd crowns, and crownets; realms and islands
          were
        As plates dropped from his pocket.
Dolabella: Cleopatra, —
Cleopatra: Think you there was, or might be, such a man,
        As this I dream'd of?
Dolabella: Gentle madam, no.
Cleopatra: You lie, up to the hearing of the gods.

What could be more effective, to render the intensity of Cleopatra's passion, and contrast it with prosaic normal life? And what could be more natural? " You lie, up to the hearing of the gods " — Cleopatra's dream — Antony is no exaggeration of the real Antony — to *her*. The implication is made superbly.

Romeo's infatuation and the romantic cast of his temperament, is similarly suggested by a love-dream.

  " If I may trust the flattering truth of sleep,
    My dreams presage some joyful news at hand:

I dreamt, my lady came and found me dead,
(Strange dream! that gives a dead man leave to think,)
And breath'd such life with kisses in my lips,
That I reviv'd, and was an emperor.
Ah me! how sweet is love itself possess'd,
When but love's shadows are so rich in joy! "

A dream is a shadow of real things; how strong
is Romeo's infatuation when he can so enjoy even
a shadow of what he hopes for. And this method
of exposition is more natural than soliloquy; and
in Shakespeare, therefore, it occurs over and over
again.

Confession and soliloquy are both subtly evaded
in the dream of Gloster (King Henry IV, I, ii),

Gloster: " My troublous dream this night doth make me sad.
Duchess: What dream'd my lord? tell me and I'll requite it
            With sweet rehearsal of my morning's dream.
Gloster: Methought this staff, mine office-badge in court,
            Was broke in twain; by whom, I have forgot,
            But, as I think, it was by the cardinal;
            And on the pieces of the broken wand
            Were plac'd the heads of Edmund Duke of
              Somerset,
            And William de la Poole, first duke of Suffolk.
            This was my dream; what it doth bode, God
              knows.
Duchess: Tut! this was nothing but an argument
            That he that breaks a stick of Gloster's grove,
            Shall lose his head for his presumption.
            But list to me, my Humphrey, my sweet duke:
            Methought I sat in seat of majesty,
            In the cathedral church of Westminster,
            And in that chair where kings and queens are
              crown'd,
            There Henry, and Dame Margaret, kneel'd to me
            And on my head did set the diadem."

Gloster then upbraids her for " hammering treach-
ery," the dream having revealed her secret wishes;
and when the Duke is murdered in his bed by
Suffolk's orders, the Cardinal cries that it is

> " God's secret judgment! — I did dream tonight
> The duke was dumb and could not speak a word."

Occult powers seem to be at work, in this profusion
of " true " dreams, and the effect is impressive.

But none of the historical plays furnishes a
better example of the inspired use of dreams than
" Henry IV, Part I," when Lady Percy makes
her dramatic appeal to Hotspur to confide in her,

> " Why hast thou lost the fresh blood in thy cheeks? . . .
> In thy faint slumbers, I by thee have watch'd,
> And heard thee murmur tales of iron wars;
> Speak terms of manage to thy bounding steed;
> Cry 'Courage! to the field.' — And thou hast talk'd
> Of sallies and retires, of trenches, tents,
> Of palisadoes, frontiers, parapets,
> Of basilisks, of cannon, culverin,
> Of prisoners' ransom, and of soldiers slain,
> And all the currents of a heady fight.
> Thy spirit within thee hath been so at war,
> And thus hast so bestirr'd thee in thy sleep,
> That beads of sweat have stood upon thy brow,
> Like bubbles in a late disturbed stream;
> And in thy face strange motions have appear'd
> Such as we see when men restrain their breath
> On some great sudden heat. Oh, what portents are
>   these?
> Some heavy business hath my lord in hand,
> And I must know it, else he loves me not."

Hotspur's obsession, his wife's concern and watchful regard, are more graphically expressed in these lines than they could have been in any other way; and the description is unmatched in dream-literature for gusto.

Mercutio's long and fantastic dissertation on dreams, in "Romeo and Juliet," scarcely adds to the intensity of the situation, but it displays to perfection his sprightly fancy, animation, and talkativeness, and affords Shakespeare an occasion to forego dramatic propriety for a moment, for a beautiful poetic digression. Romeo has had a more affecting dream than was his wont. Says Mercutio:

> " O then, I see, Queen Mab hath been with you.
> She is the fairies' midwife; and she comes
> In shape no bigger than an agate-stone
> On the forefinger of an alderman,
> Drawn with a team of little atomies
> Athwart men's noses as they lie asleep . . .
> Her chariot is an empty hazel-nut,
> Made by the joiner squirrel, or old grub,
> Time out of mind the fairies' coach-makers.
> And in this state she gallops night by night
> Through lovers' brains, and then they dream of love;
> O'er courtiers' knees, that dream on court'sies straight;
> O'er lawyers' fingers, who straight dream on fees:
> O'er ladies' lips, who straight on kisses dream,
> Which oft the angry Mab with blisters plagues,
> Because their breaths with sweetmeats tainted are:
> Sometimes she gallops o'er a courtier's nose,
> And then dreams he of smelling out a suit:
> And sometimes comes she with a tithe-pig's tail,

> Tickling a parson's nose as he lies asleep,
> Then dreams he of another benefice:
> Sometimes she driveth o'er a soldier's neck,
> And then dreams he of cutting foreign throats,
> Of breaches, ambuscadoes, Spanish blades,
> Of healths five-fathoms deep; and then anon
> Drums in his ear, at which he starts, and wakes;
> And being thus frighted, swears a pray'r or two,
> And sleeps again . . .

Romeo: Peace, peace, Mercutio, peace!
> Thou talk'st of nothing.

Mercutio: True, I talk of dreams; ?
> Which are the children of an idle brain
> Begot of nothing but vain fantasy."

No revelation here touches upon the action of the play, but the tone and movement of the description give us a concrete presentation of Mercutio's artistic and vivacious temperament.

Calpurnia's dream, in "Julius Cæsar," is of the opposite kind, and forms an integral part of the machinery of the play; it also heightens the dramatic intensity, assists the general process of suggesting fatality, and announces the intervention of supernatural powers; doom is settling over Cæsar's head, when he tells Decius his wife's dream:

> " She dream'd tonight she saw my statue,
> Which, like a fountain with a hundred spouts,
> Did run pure blood; and many lusty Romans
> Came smiling, and did bathe their hands in it:
> And these does she apply for warnings, and
>   portents,
> And evils imminent; and on her knee
> Hath begg'd that I will stay at home today.

Decius: " This dream is all amiss interpreted:
    It was a vision fair and fortunate:
    Your statue spouting blood in many pipes,
    In which so many smiling Romans bath'd,
    Signifies that from you great Rome shall suck
    Reviving blood; and that great men shall press
    For tinctures, stains, relics, and cognizance.
    This by Calpurnia's dream is signified."

The fatal plausibility of the conspirator entraps Cæsar, and we realize with overpowering alarm that his fate is sealed. The dream is a portent; and so not even supernatural warnings, it would appear, can longer save this mortal from destruction.

There is greater poignancy of feeling but less relation to the structure of the play, in the prophetic dream of Clarence, in " King Richard III." The agents are already despatched to murder him; meanwhile, in dreadful apprehension, Clarence tells his horrid dream to Brakenbury, the Governor of the Tower.

Brakenbury: " What was your dream, my lord? I pray you,
        tell me.
Clarence: Methought that I had broken from the Tower
        And was embark'd to cross to Burgundy;
        And in my company, my brother Gloster:
        Who from my cabin tempted me to walk
        Upon the hatches: thence we look'd toward
          England . . .
        . . . As we pac'd along
        Upon the giddy footing of the hatches,
        Methought that Gloster stumbled, and, in fall-
          ing,

Struck me, that thought to stay him, over-
        board,
Into the tumbling billows of the main.
O Lord! methought what pain it was to
        drown! . . .
Methought I saw a thousand fearful wrecks . . .
Wedges of gold, great anchors, heaps of pearl,
Inestimable stones, unvalu'd jewels,
All scatter'd in the bottom of the sea:
    . . . the envious flood
Stopt in my soul, and would not let it forth
To find the empty, vast, and wandering air;
But smother'd it within my panting bulk,
Which almost burst to belch it in the sea.

Brakenbury: Awak'd you not with this sore agony?
Clarence: No, no, my dream was lengthened after life;
I pass'd, methought, the melancholy flood,
With that grim ferryman that poets write of,
Unto the kingdom of perpetual night.
The first that there did greet my stranger soul
Was   my   great   father-in-law,   renowned
        Warwick;
Who cried aloud, ' What scourge for perjury
Can this dark monarchy afford false Clarence? '
And so he vanish'd: then came wandering by
A shadow like an angel, with bright hair
Dabbled in blood; and he shrieked out aloud,
' Clarence is come, — false, fleeting, perjur'd
        Clarence, —
That stabb'd me in the field by Tewkesbury; —
Seize on him, Furies! take him to your tor-
        ments! '
With that, methought, a legion of foul fiends
Environ'd me, and howled in mine ears
Such hideous cries, that, with the very noise,
I trembling wak'd, and, for a season after,
Could not believe but that I was in hell,
Such terrible impression made my dream."

The conscience-stricken prisoner, apprehensive of

the future, and remorseful for the past, is portrayed with overwhelming pathos. The poetry, the dream, the situation, lend one another support, and here, as a vehicle for conveying overpowering emotion, the dream is employed by Shakespeare in a form that is unsurpassed, even by Dostoievsky in Raskolnikoff's dream of the mare killed by an axe, shortly before he himself murdered the old pawnbrokeress with the selfsame instrument.*

Dreams almost as intense, though not so portentous, appall Mr. Holdforth in his ghastly night at Wuthering Heights. In the first, a horrid monotony oppressed his spirits. " In my dream, Jabes had a full and attentive congregation; and he preached — good God! what a sermon: divided into *four hundred and ninety* parts, each fully equal to an ordinary address from the pulpit, and each discussing a separate sin! " The congregation stormed. " Presently the whole chapel resounded with rappings and counter-rappings; every man's hand was against his neighbour; and Brandenham, unwilling to remain idle, poured forth his zeal in a shower of loud taps on the boards of the pulpit, which responded so smartly that, at last, to my unspeakable relief, they woke me. And what was it that had suggested the tremendous tumult? What had played Jabes' part in the row? Merely, the branch of a fir-tree that touched my lattice

* " Crime and Punishment."

as the blast wailed by, and rattled its dry cones against my panes! "

But the second following hard upon this last, contains still more " the fierce vexation of a dream." " I heard the bough repeat its teasing sound, and ascribed it to the right cause; but it annoyed me so much that I resolved to silence it, if possible; and, I thought, I rose and endeavoured to unhasp the casement. The hook was soldered into the casement; a circumstance observed by me when awake, but forgotten. ' I must stop it nevertheless! ' I muttered, knocking my knuckles thro' the glass, and stretching an arm out to seize the importunate branch; instead of which my fingers closed on the fingers of a little, ice-cold hand! The intense horror of nightmare came over me; I tried to draw back my arm, but the hand clung to it, and a most melancholy voice sobbed, ' Let me in — let me in! ' ' Who are you? ' I asked, struggling, meanwhile, to disengage myself. ' Catherine Linton,' it replied shiveringly; ' I'm come home; I'd lost my way on the moor! ' As it spoke, I discerned, obscurely, a child's face looking through the window. Terror made me cruel; and, finding it useless to attempt shaking the creature off, I pulled its wrist on to the broken pane, and rubbed it to and fro till the blood ran down and soaked the bedclothes; still it wailed, ' Let me in! ' and maintained its tenacious gripe, almost mad-

dening me with fear . . . ' Begone!' I shouted,
' I'll never let you in, not if you beg for twenty
years!' ' It is twenty years,' mourned the voice,
' twenty years. I've been a waif for twenty
years!' I tried to jump up; but could not stir a
limb; and so yelled aloud in a frenzy of fright."

A much commoner usage in literature is for the
dream-idea to serve as a frame work or peg, within
which to set, or upon which to hang a fantastical,
revolutionary, or unmotived story. Or it may
form only a part of the plot machinery, without
being the sole excuse for the story's existence.

A revolutionary manifesto would not only call
down upon itself the terrors of the law, but would,
in its harsh attack upon existing prejudices,
alienate many of its possible convertites; but
presented in the pleasant form of a dream, or
romance, it may disarm both the law and prejudice,
and reach even those who share the popular dis-
taste for abstruse treatises and abstract questions.
And so a dream of this sort forms a popular
dramatization of ideas resisted by the censor of
public opinion.

Langland, indignant with the social and religious
systems of his time, the corrupt church and class
tyranny of the fourteenth century, wrote his
attack on them in the disguised form of a dream
allegory, " The Vision of Piers Plowman," which
would enable him both to avoid prosecution, and

present his ideas in an easy and palatable form. The poem opens with the celebrated alliterative lines:

> " In a summer season, when soft was the sun,
> In rough cloth I robed me, as I a shepherd were,
> In habit like an hermit in his works unholy,
> And through the wide world I went, wonders to hear.
> But on a May morning, on Malvern hills,
> A marvel befell me — sure from fancy it came —
> I had wandered me weary, so weary, I rested me
> On a broad bank by a merry-sounding burn;
> And as I lay and leaned and looked into the waters
> I slumbered in a sleeping, it rippled so merrily,
> And I dreamed — marvellously.
> All the world's weal, all the world's woe,
> Truth and trickery, treasure and guile,
> All I saw, sleeping."*

Under a similar guise, " The Pilgrim's Progress " presented to a public fond of exciting stories the unpopular Puritan views of Christian duty. " As I walked," the book opens, " through the wilderness of this world, I lighted on a certain place where was a den; and I laid me down in that place to sleep: and as I slept I dreamed a dream. I dreamed, and behold I saw a man clothed with rags, standing in a certain place, with his face from his own house, a book in his hand, and a great burden upon his back. I looked and saw him open the book and read therein; and as he read he wept and trembled: and, not being able

* Modernized version, by Arthur Burrell.

longer to contain, he brake out with a lamentable cry, saying, What shall I do? "

Plato dreamed his utopian " Republic." It was in a vision that Dante visited Purgatory, Inferno and Paradise. The " Faerie Queene " is substantially a fragment of a series of dreams. Cicero taught his philosophy of a future life in " The Dream of Scipio." In this last the ghost of Scipio Africanus appears to Cicero, and declares that those who on earth labor for the public good will go after death to an abode of bliss. Chaucer, reading in this book one night as he lay in bed, fell off to sleep, and began to dream —

> " How African, right in that selfe aray
> That Scipioun him saw before that tyde
> Was comen, and stood right at my beddes syde."

Then Scipio conducted Chaucer to the Parliament of Birds, where he heard an allegorical debate.

Leigh Hunt enshrines his humanitarian gospel in the vision of " Abou Ben Adhem "; the angel is to write him down, not as " one who loves the Lord," but " as one who loves his fellow man "; yet when the list is shown to him,

"Lo! Ben Adhem's name led all the rest."

The dream may, on the other hand, play but a secondary rôle in the work. In " The Dream " by Ivan Turgenev, the narrator has a vision of a man who pays a visit, under mysterious circumstances, to a certain house, that is very clearly distinguished in all its details. Next day, to his surprise the dreamer sees in real life a man of the same appearance enter an exactly similar house. Some days elapse, and then the narrator has a second dream, in which he sees the man lying dead at a certain point on the beach; next day he goes to the place and truly enough sees a body lying exactly as in the dream. It turned out to be the body of his father. Unity and interest are thus imparted to a not very tractable or exciting series of incidents by the subordinate idea of two dreams. In a somewhat similar way, Charles Cothill, in Masefield's race romance " Right Royal " dreams that his horse appears before him and declares that he will win the race. " It is my day," he shouts. By this device we are led to take a more than ordinary interest in Right Royal's chances.

" Peter Ibbetson," a rather wild and unreal novel by George du Maurier, contains a dream interest, though on a far larger scale: unity is lent to it by a dream motive. Peter is a morbid agnostic, who finds compensation in dreams for the limited and monotonous life he is forced to lead during the day with his limited means.

The Duchess of Towers — formerly his playmate at Passy, near Paris — dreams too, and a strange community of soul springs up between them; for Peter and the Duchess dream of each other simultaneously, their dreams becoming united and as real as life, so that they are able to carry on a secret but active friendship in their sleep, precisely analogous to the waking friendship of ordinary mortals. Their uncanny form of dream is induced by sleeping on the back, with the arms crossed under the head, and the right foot lying over the left.

Peter is sent to gaol and there he carries on his friendship with the Duchess for twenty-five years, until it is broken off by the death of the Duchess, when the dreams come abruptly to an end, and Peter goes mad. Yet in the asylum to which he is sent, he carries on some sort of communication with his beloved, in spirit dreams.

Peter's dreams were extraordinary in another way, too. The Duchess and he build a house together, supplying the several parts from the finest palaces in Europe — after the manner of Abbotsford.

Also, whenever and wherever the Duchess goes abroad, the books, pictures, plays, music, operas, and sights of her travels, are all faithfully conveyed in dreams to Peter, who, as it were, travels all the time with her. Each of the dreamers is a composite self, of himself or herself and all direct ancestors. Any moment of the past can be evoked at pleasure, merely by a transformation for the moment into whatever ancestor lived at the given time.

A very different order of dreams is that (already mentioned on the great scale — like " The Pilgrim's Progress ") in which an essayist, when healing with philosophical ideas, supposes himself to fall asleep in his meditations, and to behold the ideas, in mimic dramatic guise, rise up and perform a little dumb show. Addison closes his series of essays on " Wit " in this way,* introducing the device by an explanation that " it is very hard for the mind to disengage itself from a subject in which it has been long employed. It is to this that I impute my last night's dream or vision, which formed into one continued allegory the several schemes of wit, whether false, mixed or true, that have been the subject of my late papers. Methought I was transported into a country that was filled with prodigies and enchantments, governed by the goddess of Falsehood, and entitled the Region of False Wit." He then presents a fantasy that would be intolerable as hard fact, but which, in the form of a dream, composes an illuminating illustration.

Lamb has written one or two essays in the same vein, neither true dreams nor pure allegories, but burlesques. In " A Vision of Horns " he supposes that men have horns growing out of their foreheads, and offers plausible reasons to account for their rich variety. In " The Child Angel: A Dream,"

* " The Spectator," Nos. 58, 59, 60 and 63.

he pretends to have gone to bed one night with his head full of speculations upon " The Loves of the Angels," a book he had been reading. Transported in a dream to a celestial region, he there encountered a Child-Angel, dressed in swaddling-clothes; budding wings appeared on its white shoulders; and, as the years rolled by in myriads (for " in dreams Time is nothing "), the Child-Angel continued unchanged, refusing like Peter Pan to grow up, and became Tutelar Genius of Children on Earth.

This, of course, in no way ends the different methods in which dreams are employed as a device or as a subject in literature; but it is sufficient to show what an important place the dream occupies, and how ill could be replaced. The subject could be indefinitely extended by taking into account rites, customs, and myths, connected with the dream idea, and showing how far the human imagination in those aspects is dependent on the dream process for obtaining its sustenance.

But here we will call a halt. The old dream devices will be used again and again in the future, for they are permanent and flexible; dreams will again be the motive for stories and the excuse for fantasies; but, above all, great advances will yet be made in our conception of the dream and its functions, and then literature will faithfully reflect them, and use them for purposes of her own. As long as literature exists, so long will dreams remain a portion of its machinery as well as a subject in itself.

THE END

INDEX

INDEX

Greenlanders, dreams according to, 17.

HALLUCINATIONS, the nature of, 2.
Hallowe'en, customs of, in County Leitrim, 65, 66; in the Hebrides, 66.
Hamlet, irresolution of, 118; play within the play of, 137, 187.
Hashish, dreams stimulated by, 95.
Hazlitt, on continuous dreaming, 100, 195; on wish-fulfilment, 197, 198.
Hawthorne, Nathaniel, 193.
Hecuba, the dream of, 42.
Hearn, Lafcadio, 190.
Héger, M., in novels of Charlotte Brontë, 190.
Hippocrates, dreams according to, 46.
Holdforth, Mr. in *Wuthering Heights*, 231–233.
Homer, dreams in, 37.
Hood, Thomas, the *Whims and Oddities* of, 6.
Hotspur, Harry, Shakespeare's, 226.
Horses, dreams of, 9.
Hunt, Leigh, 235.

IMPULSIVE, people by nature, 177.
Im Thurm, on the Indians in Guiana, 18.
Incubation, advantages of, 58; amongst the Greeks, 59–61; method of, 59.
Indians, ancestor dreams of, 19; Big Belly, war oracle of, 65.
Ingimund, travel dream ordered by, 64.
Interest, meaning of technical term, 177.
Isaiah, 194.

JEWS, dream-theories of, 35, 79–81.
Joseph, dreams of the Biblical, 32.
Jung, Dr. C. G., association test of, 152; word-list of, 152, 153; use of word-list of, 154; types of answers to word-list of, 157. See also under Freud.
Jung, Dr. Henri, of Zürich, on dream superstitions, 81.

KARENS, dream-scenery according to the, 24.
Keats, John, 191.
Kimmins, Dr., classifications of children's dreams by, 139–141.
Krauss, lunar dream of, 92, 93.
Kubla Khan, origin of, 218–221.

LACTANTIUS, dreams according to, 50.
Ladd, Prof., on Bergson's theory, 101.
Lamb, Charles, dreams of, 195, 198–202, 238, 239.
Lancet, on Freud, 165.
Langland, John, the *Piers Plowman* of, 233, 234.
Lebadea, oracle of, 61.
Length of dreams, 8.
Libido, nature of, 177.
London, Jack, on partially clothed dream, 102; on falling dream, 102, 103.

INDEX